I0479224

The fantasy coloring book

BY OSCAR BELTRÁN

Wild animals

1ST EDITION

Welcome to the fascinating world of animal life! This coloring book brings you an amazing collection of high-quality animal designs, designed to satisfy animal and color therapy lovers.

Each page of this coloring book features detailed and unique designs of animals in different poses and situations that reflect each one's unique personality. The designs include a wide variety of animals, from farm animals to wild animals, and feature a wide variety of coloring styles and designs.

This coloring book is perfect for animal lovers, color therapy enthusiasts, and those who enjoy relaxation and creativity. Use your colored pencils or watercolors to bring each design to life and create your own work of art.

This coloring book is ideal for children and adults, and is a great way to share a moment of relaxation and creativity with friends and family.

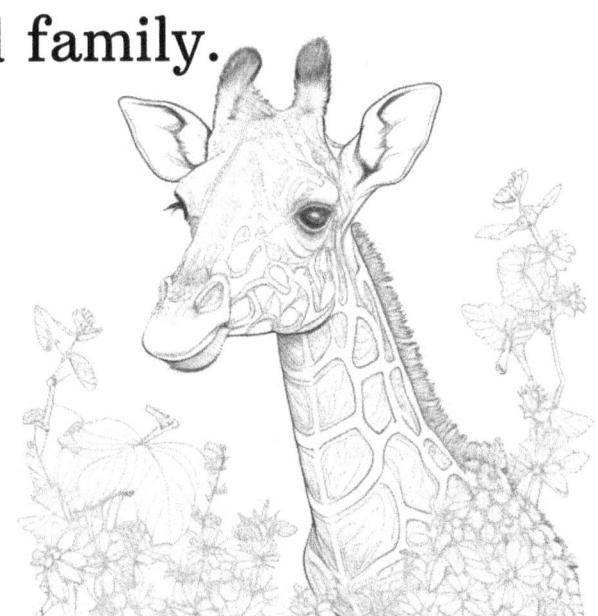

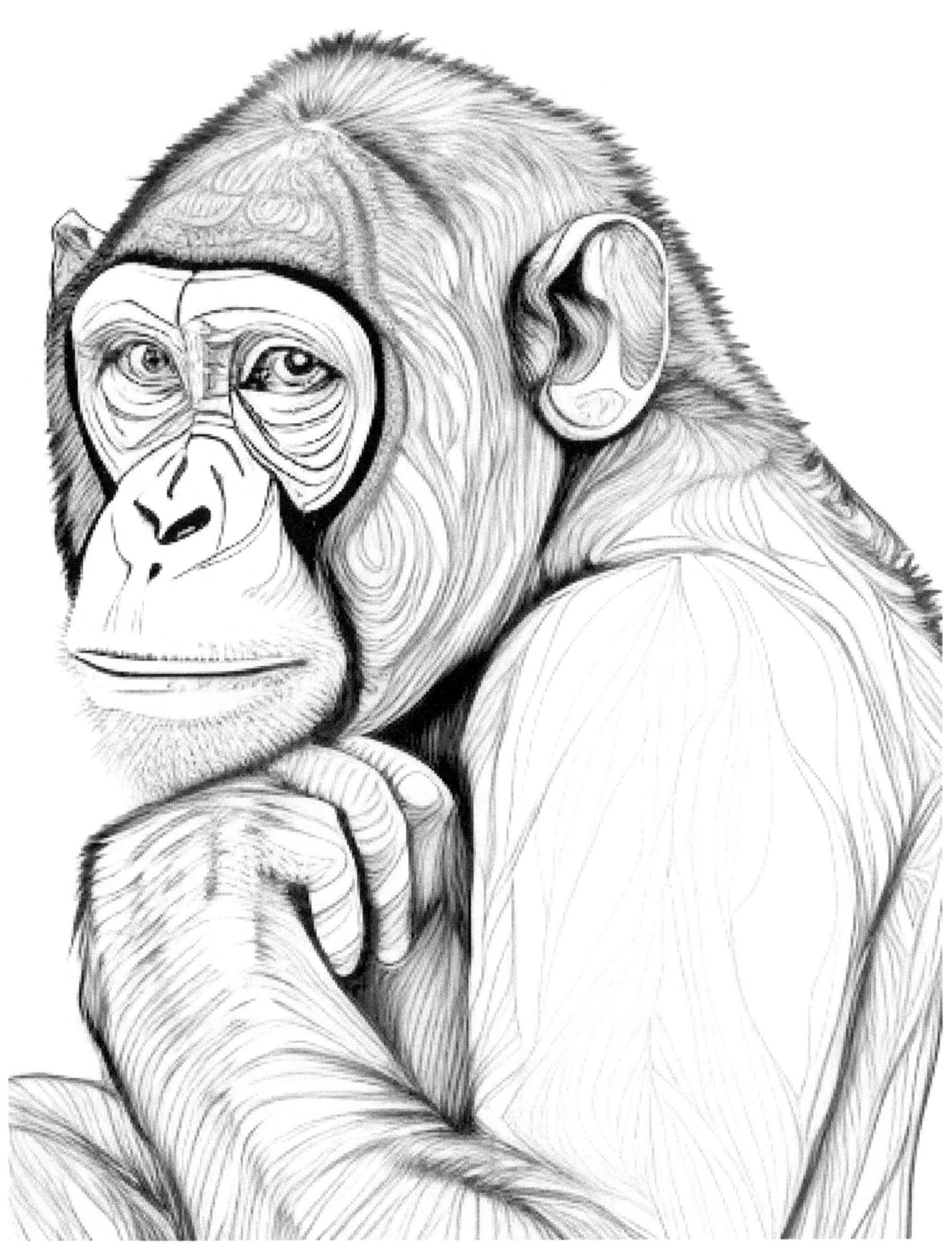

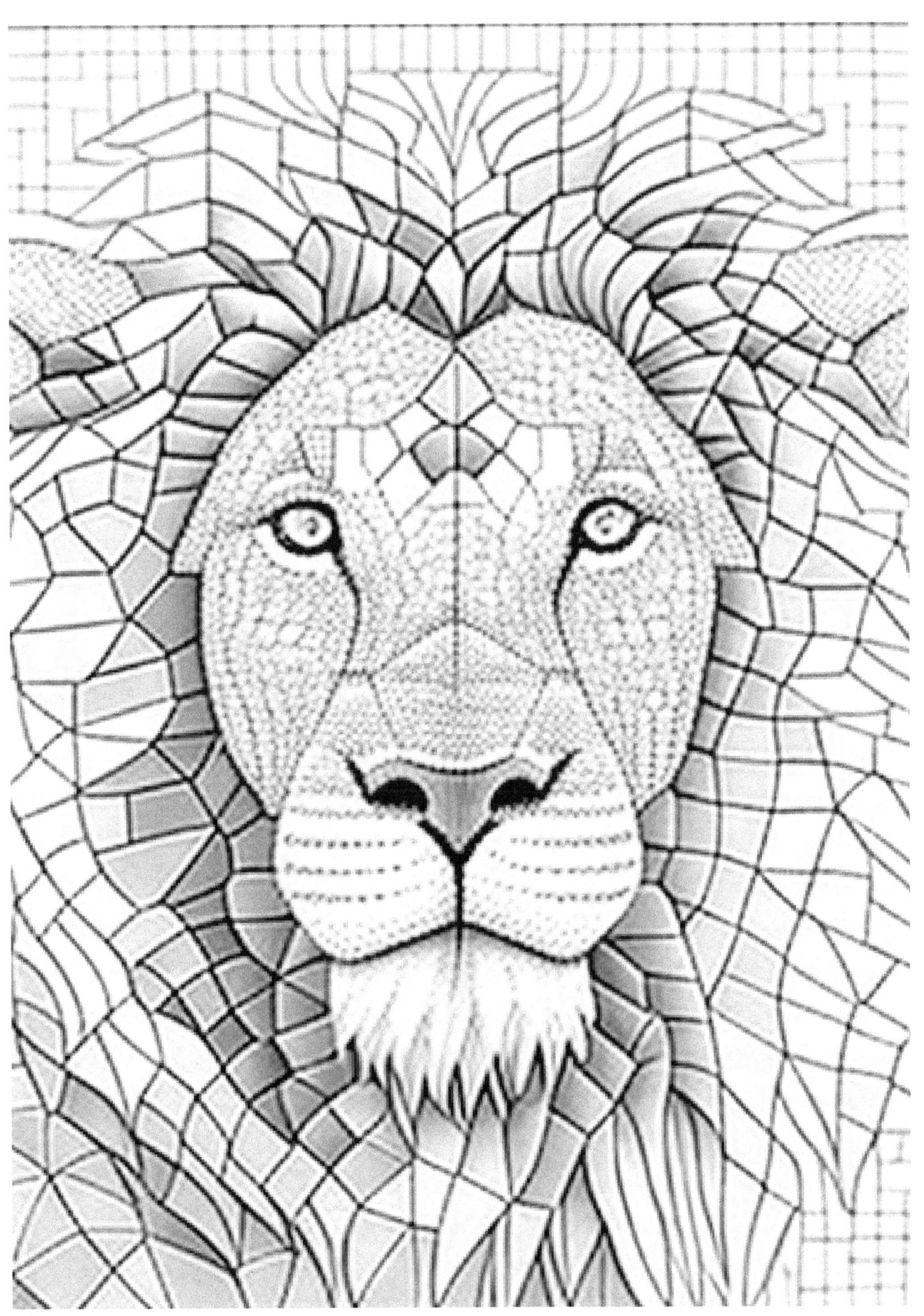

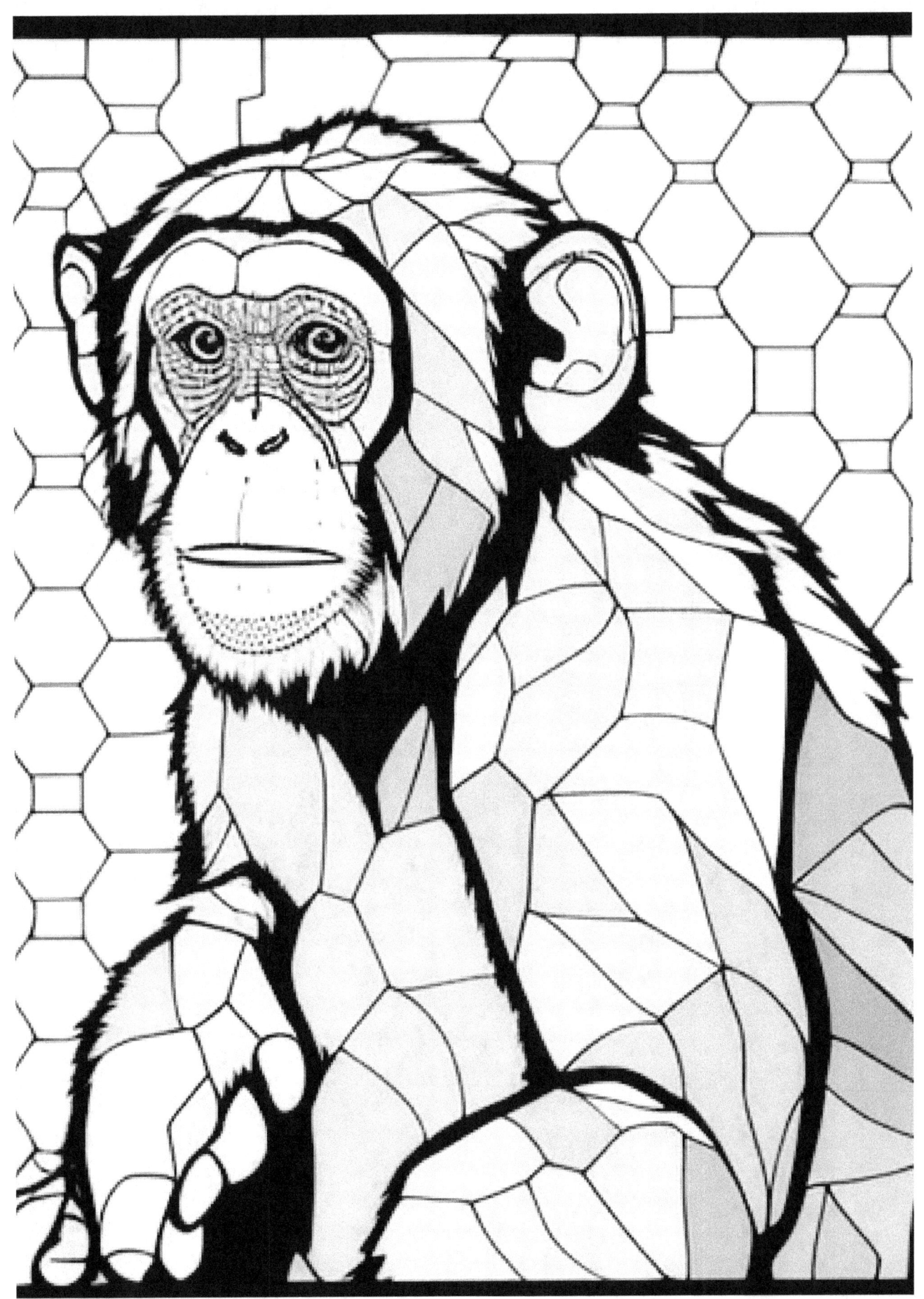

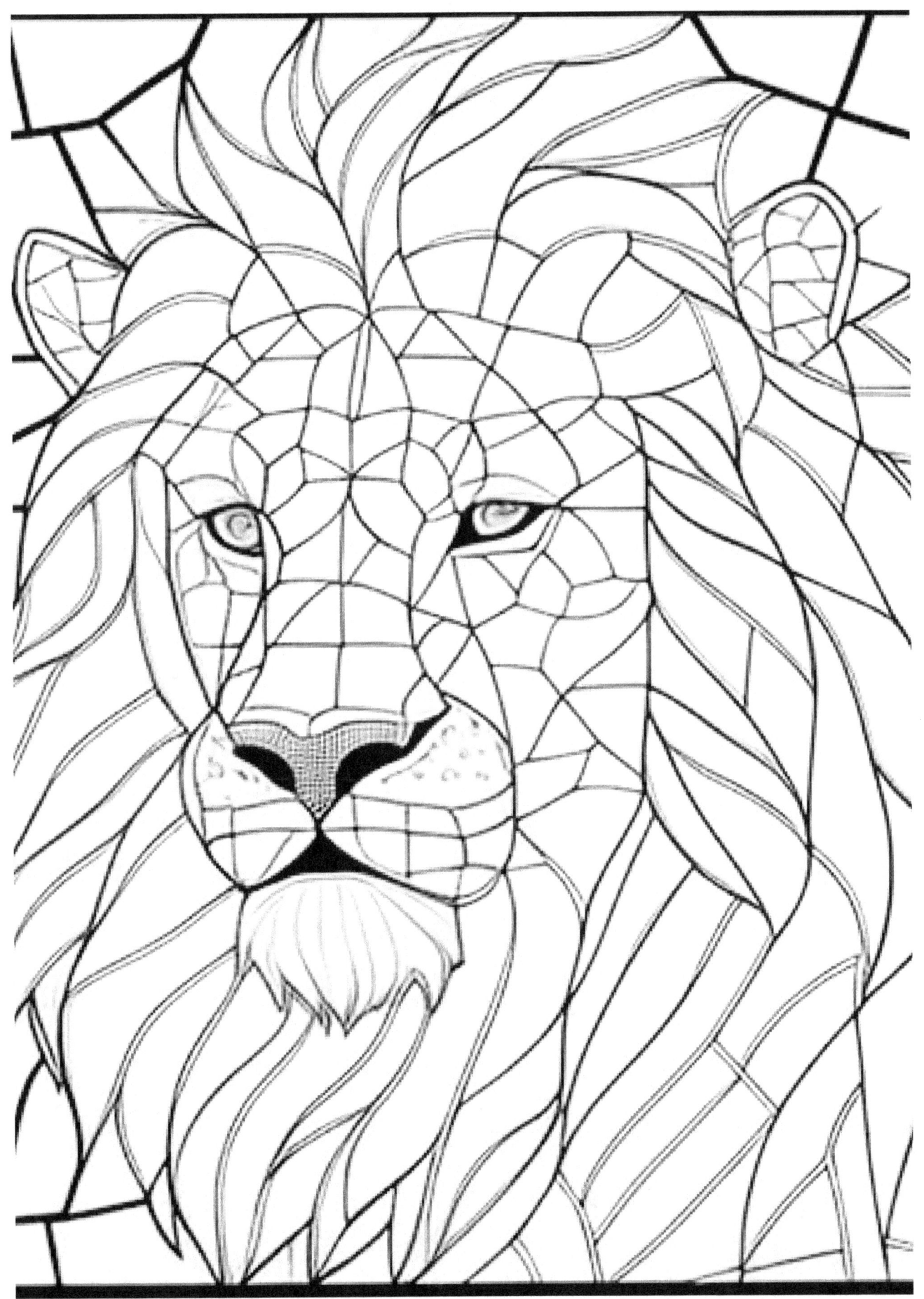

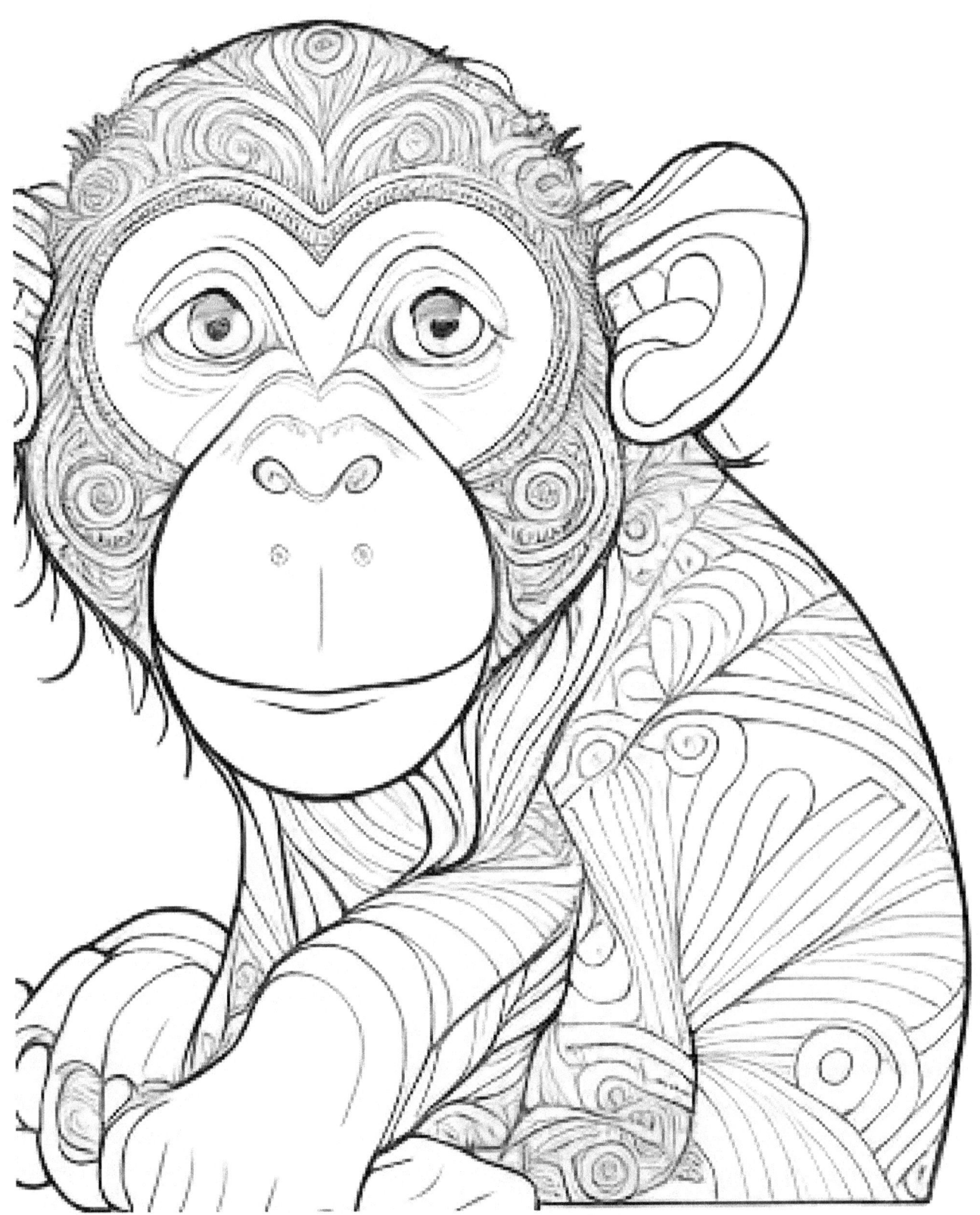

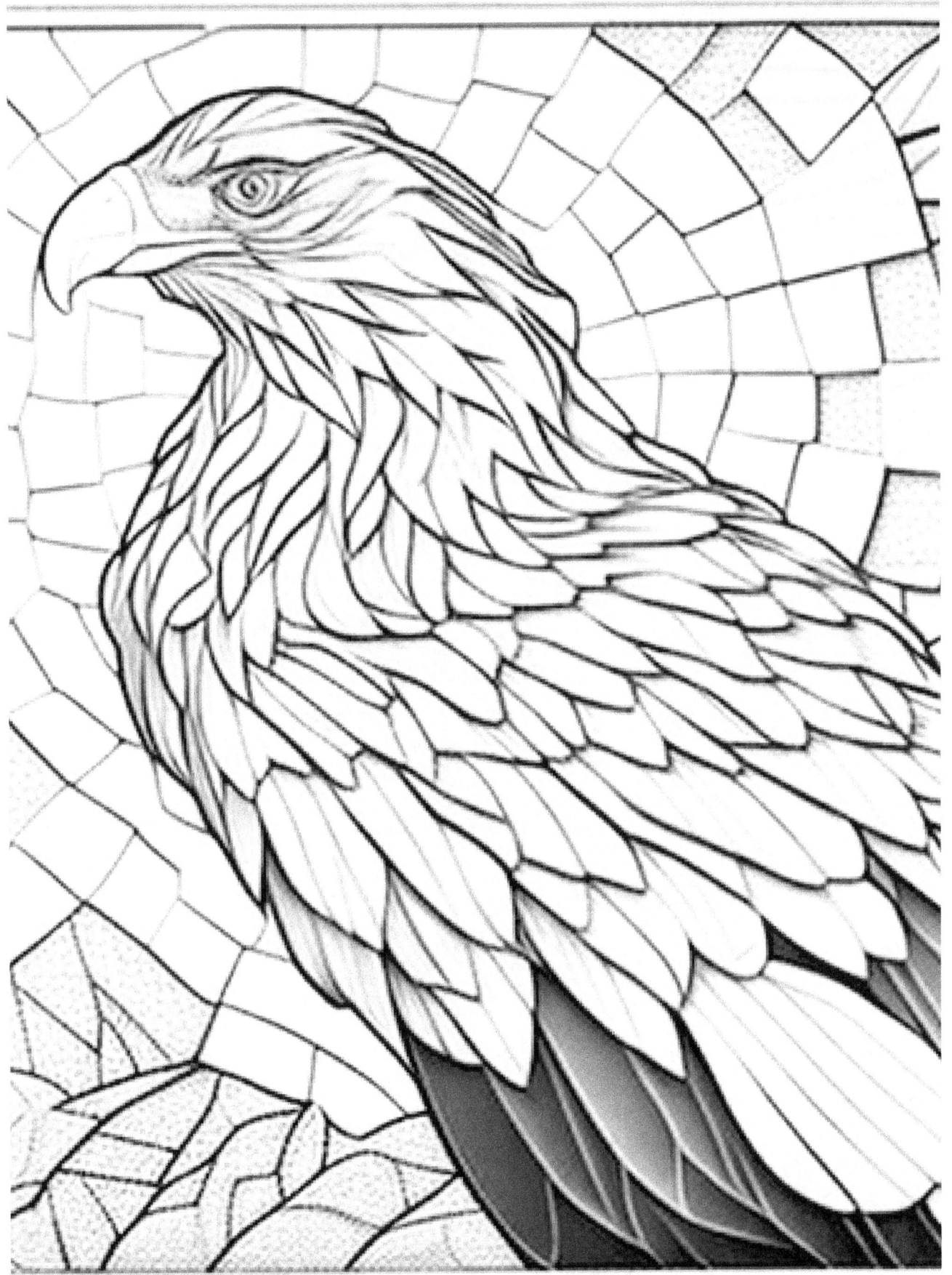

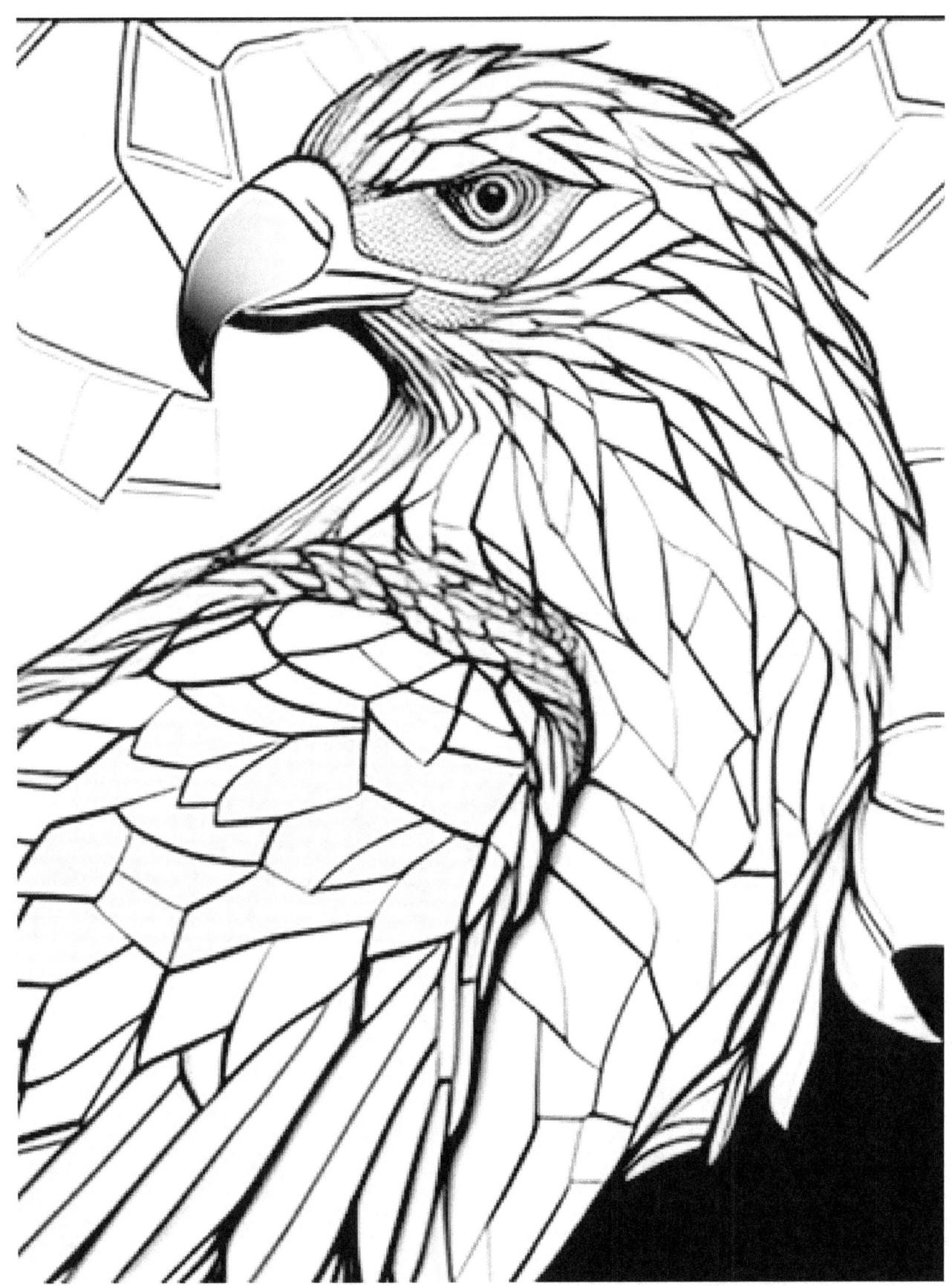

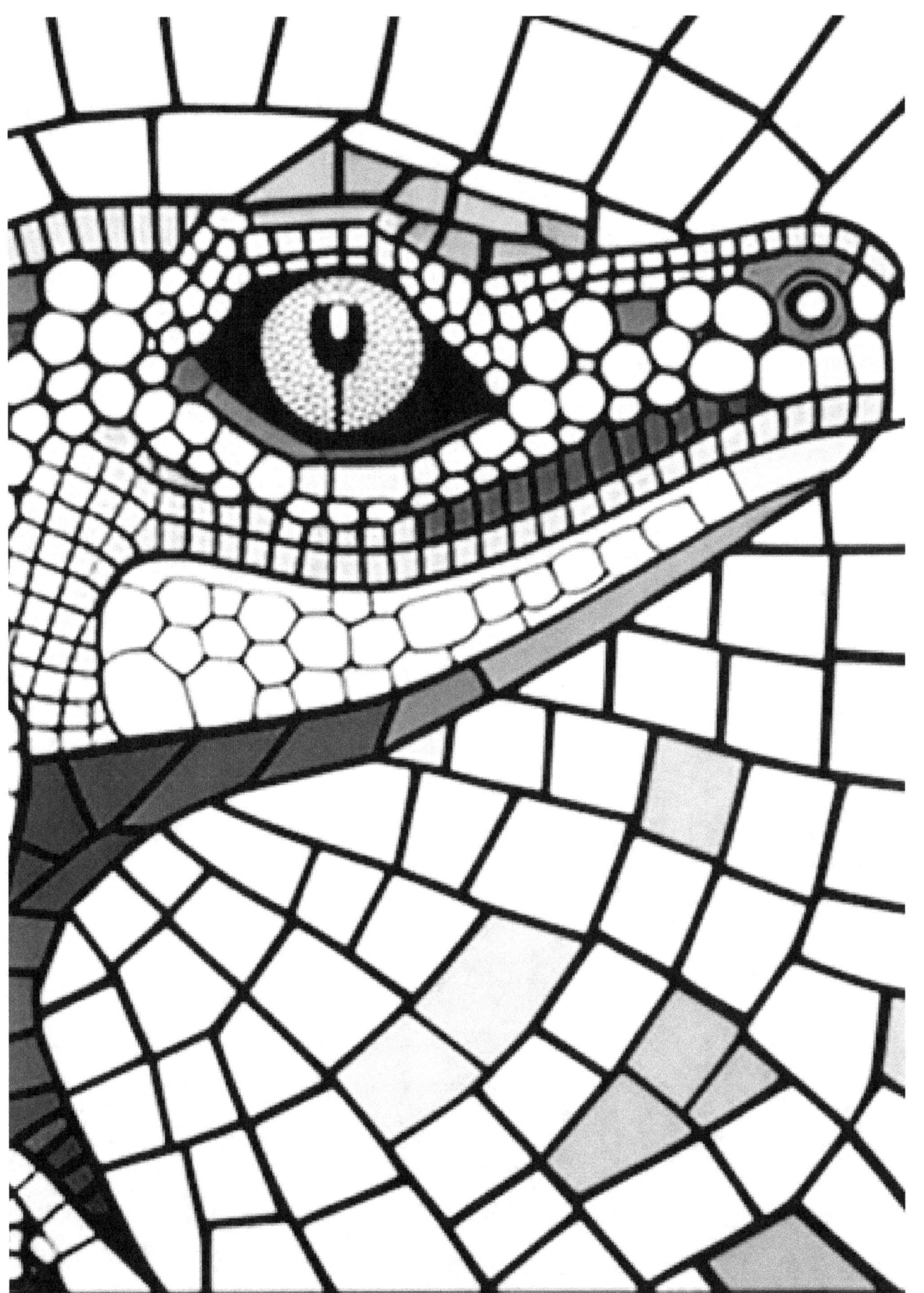

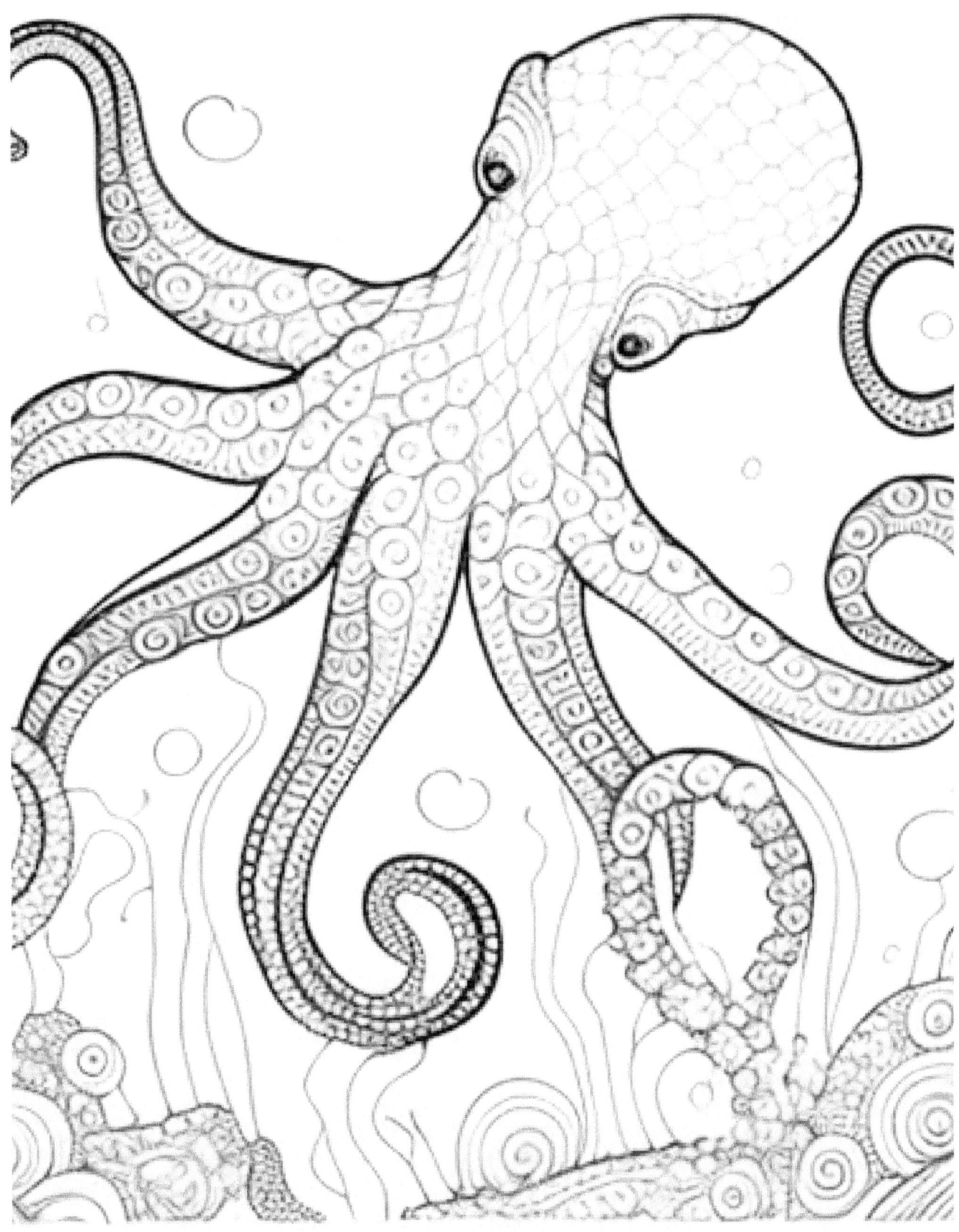

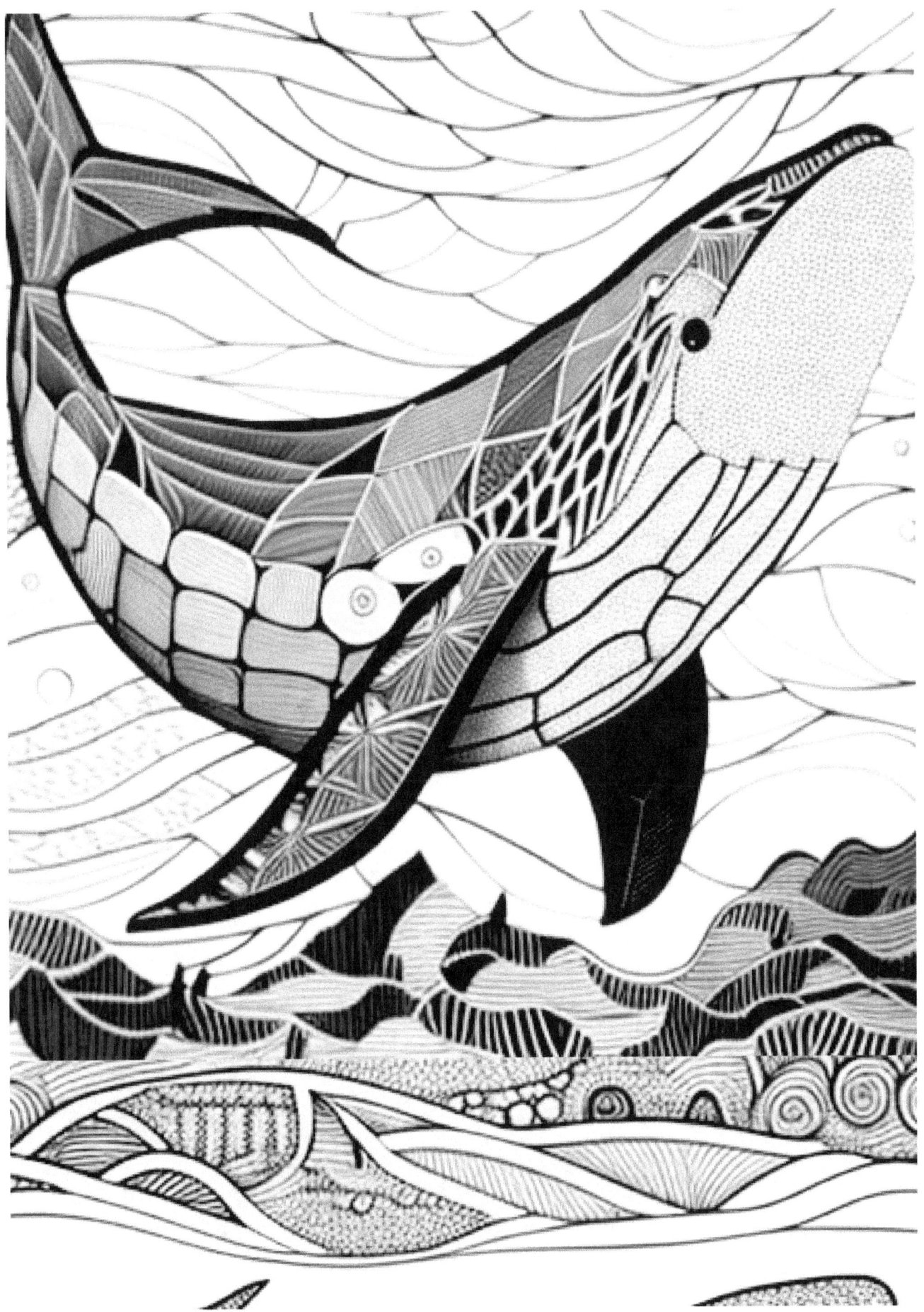

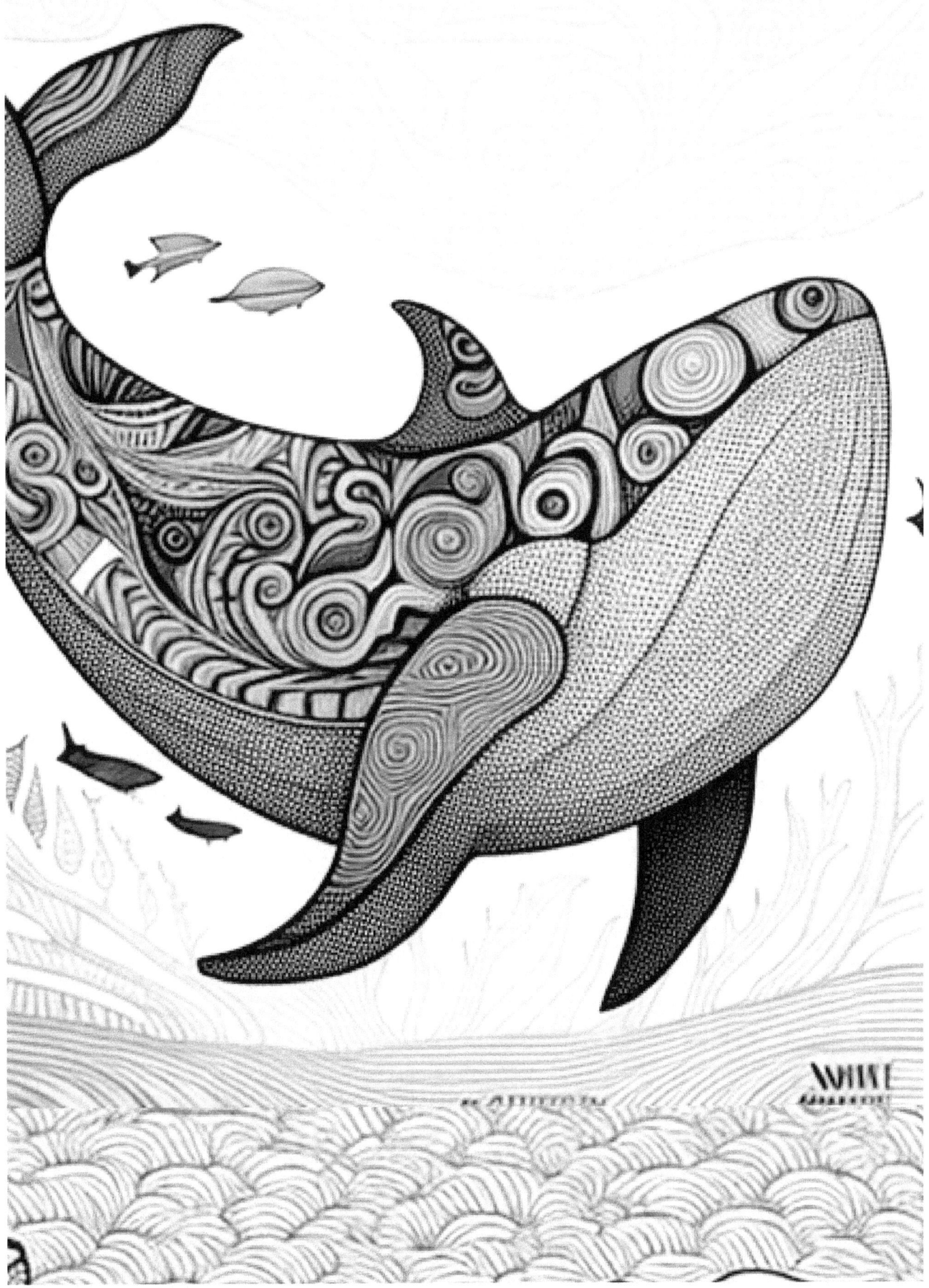

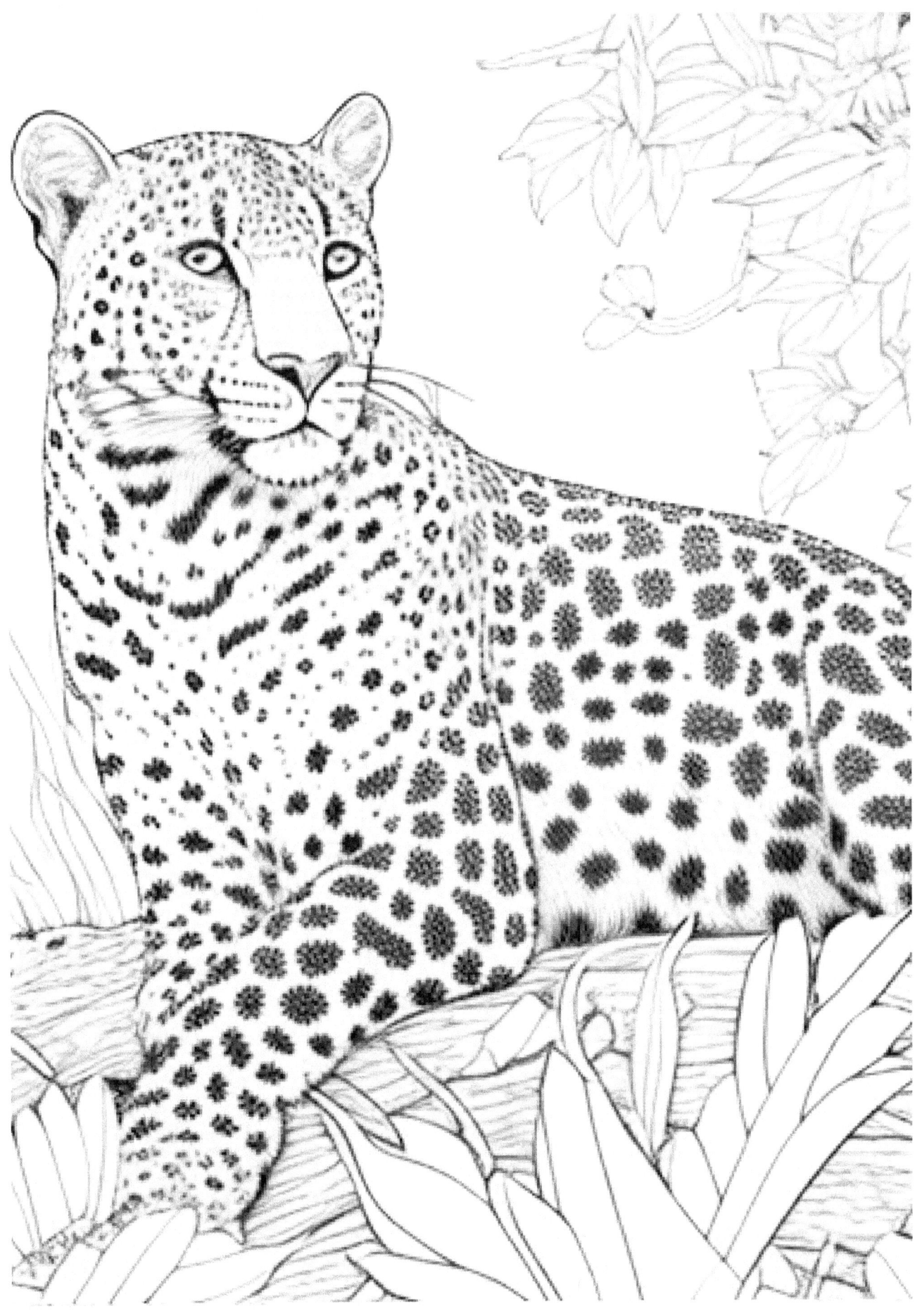

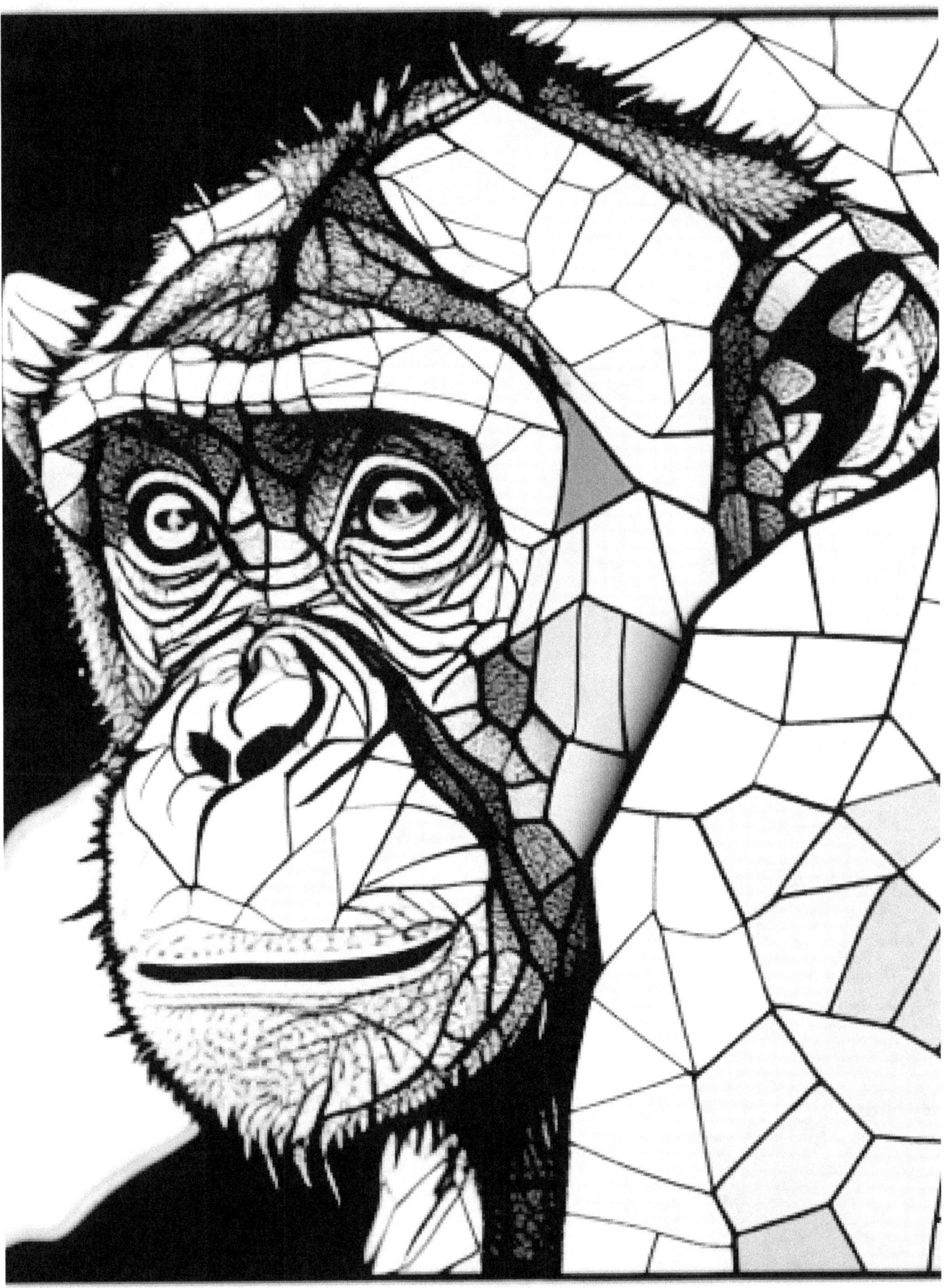

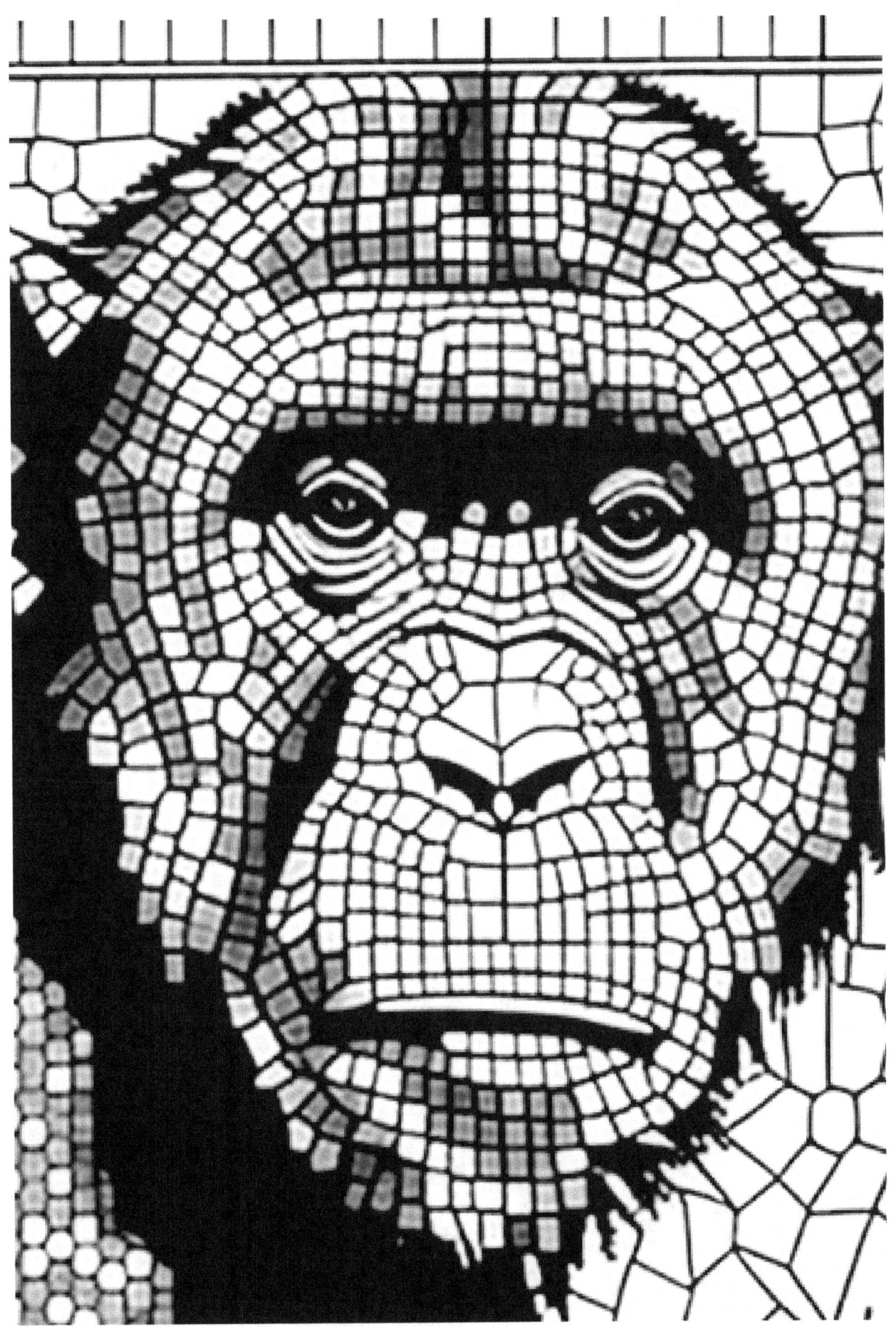

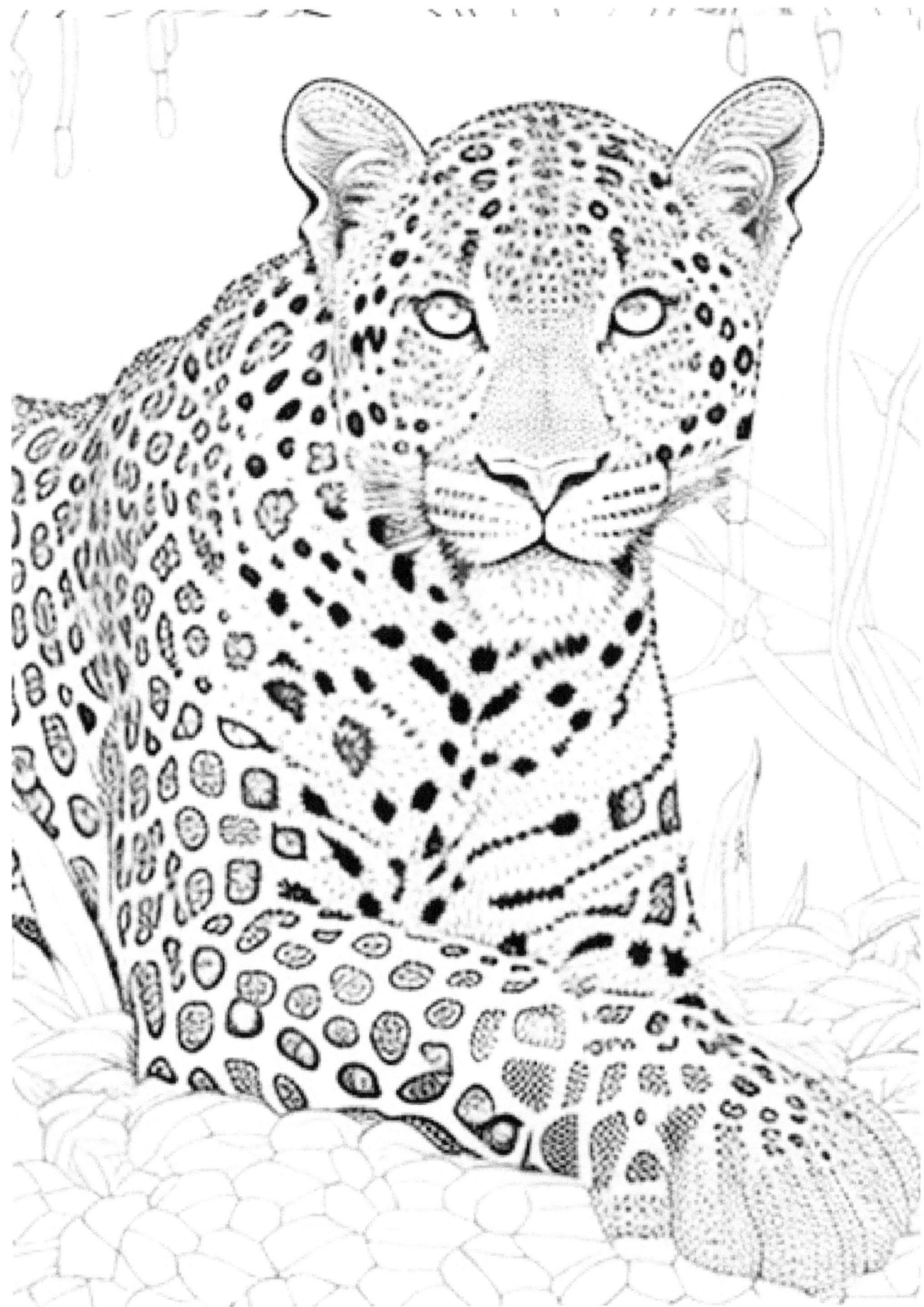

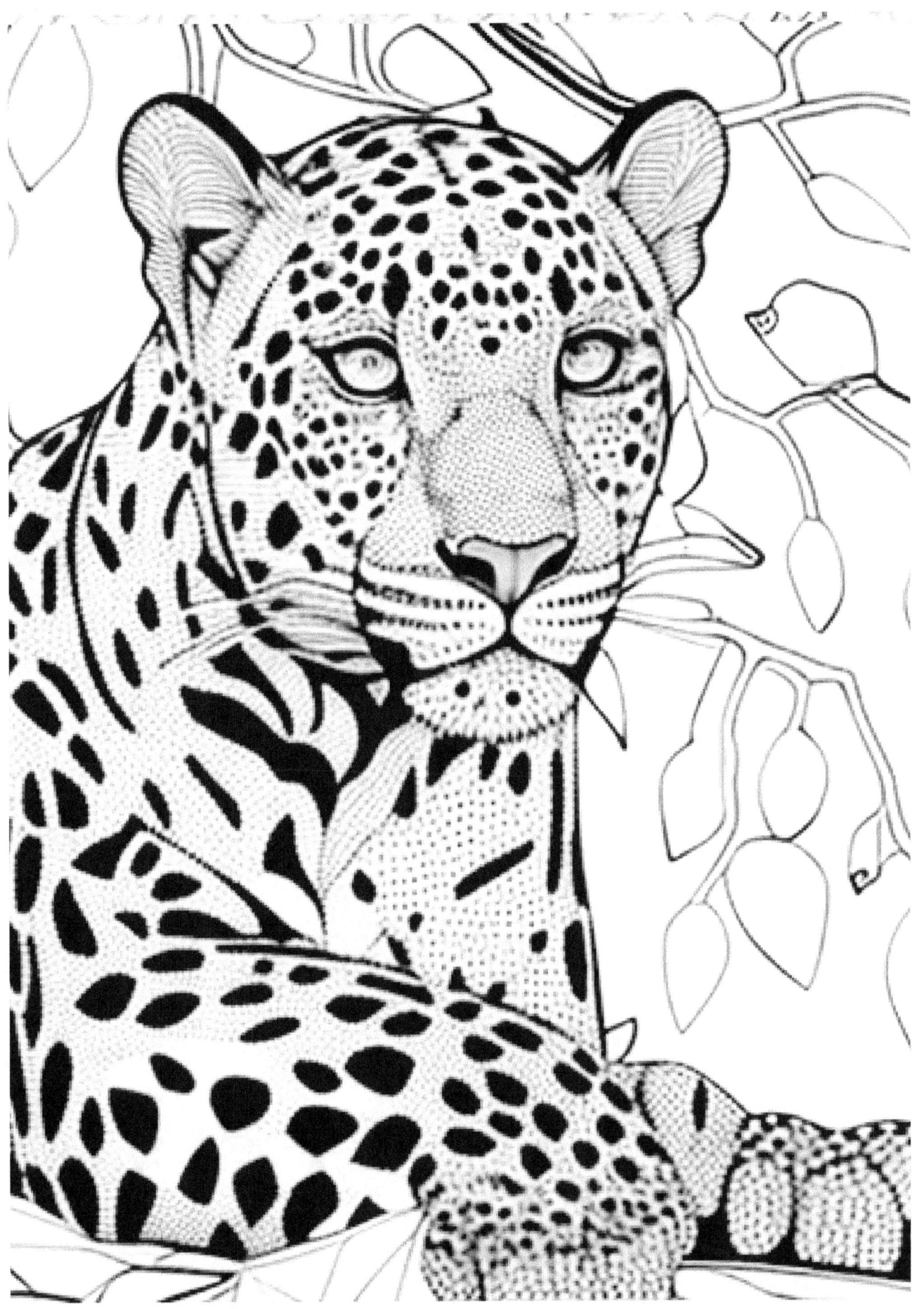

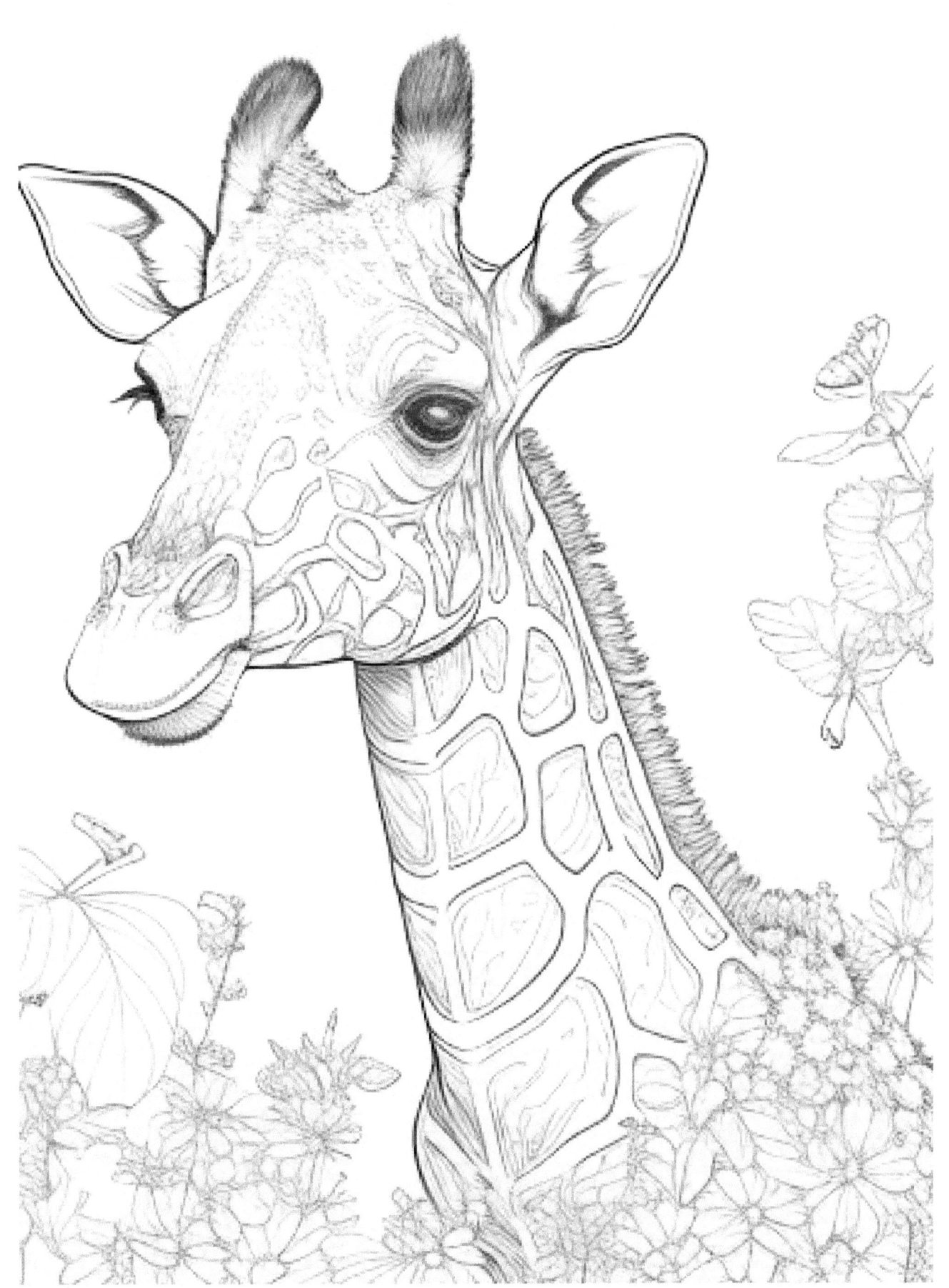

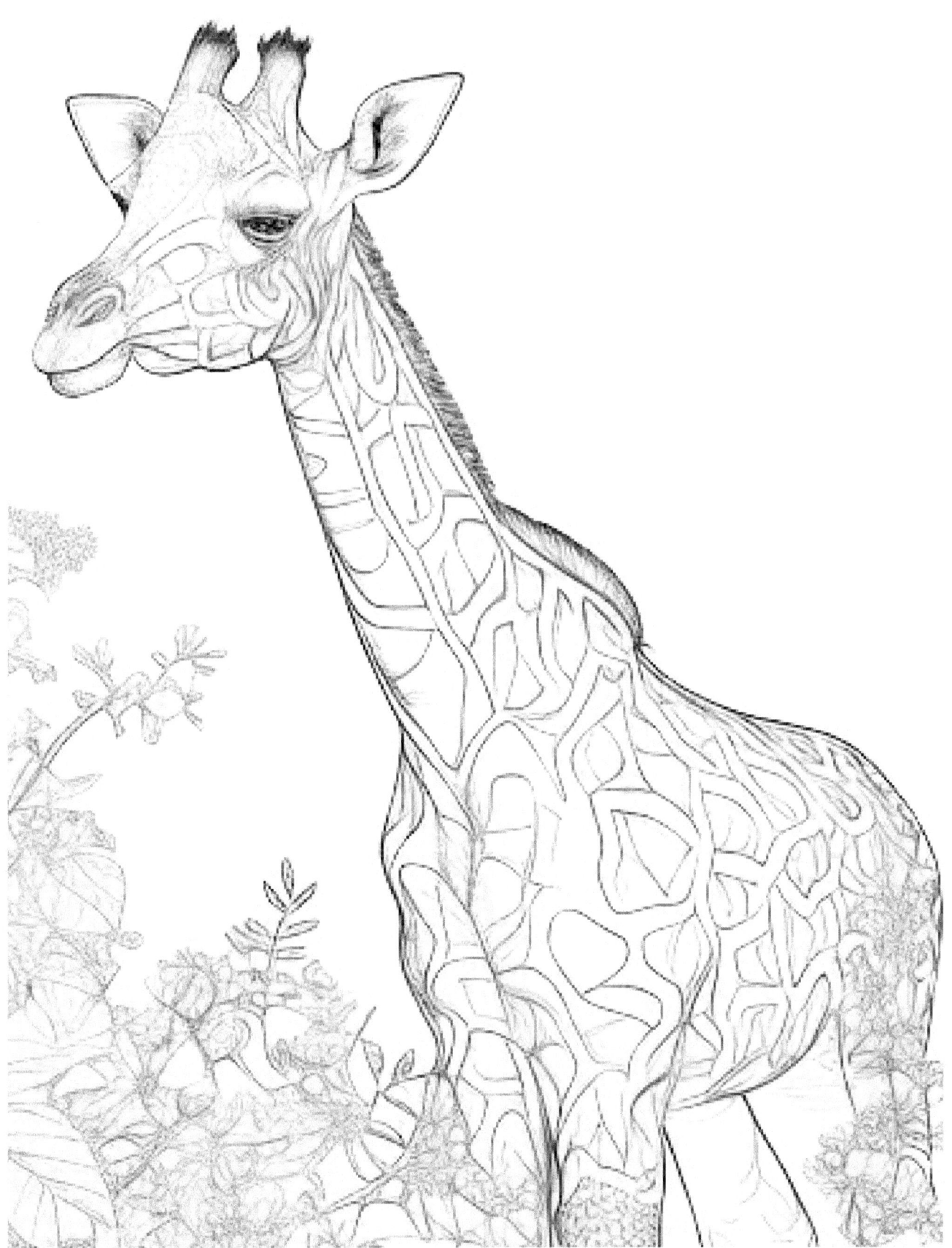

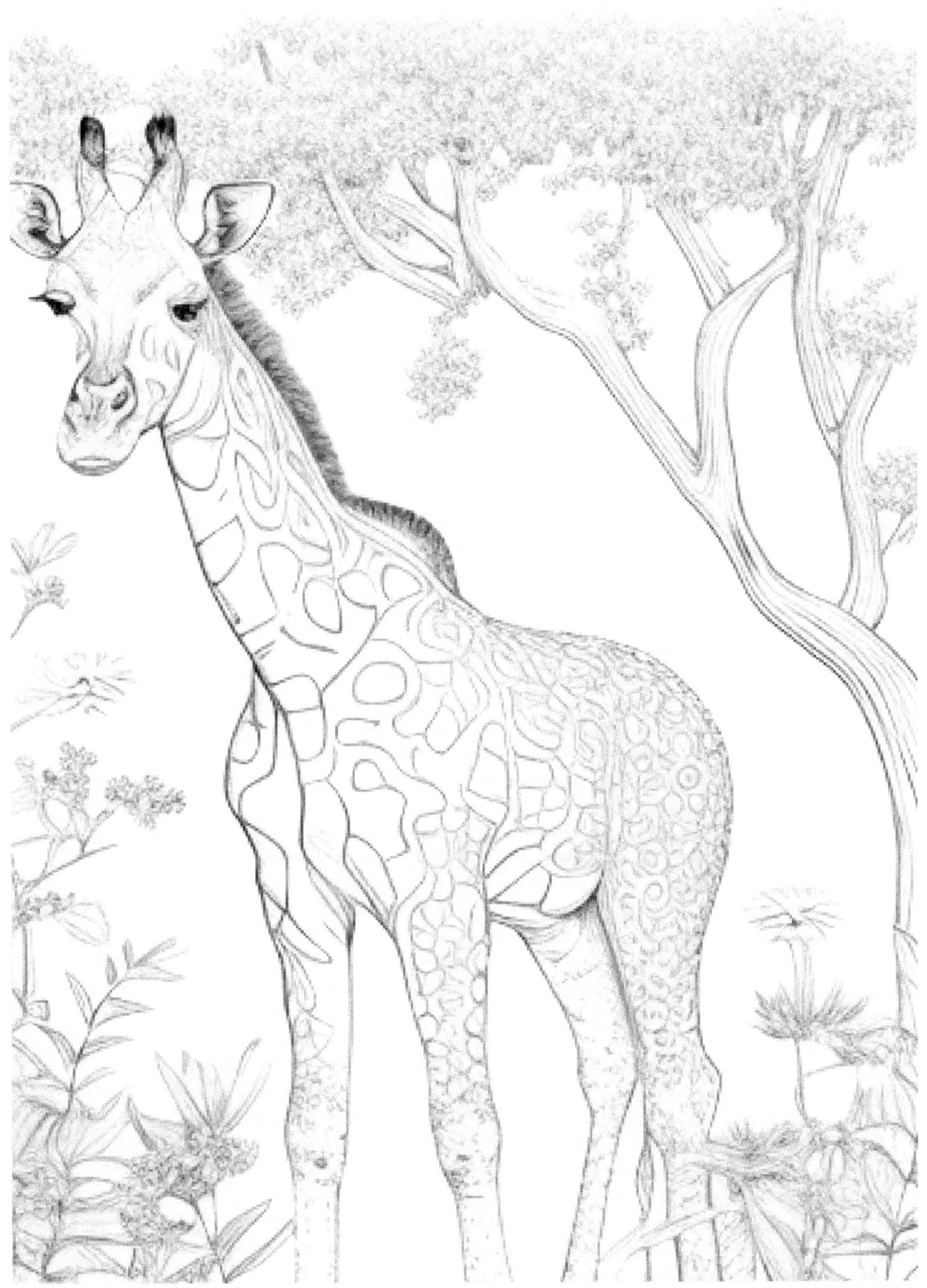

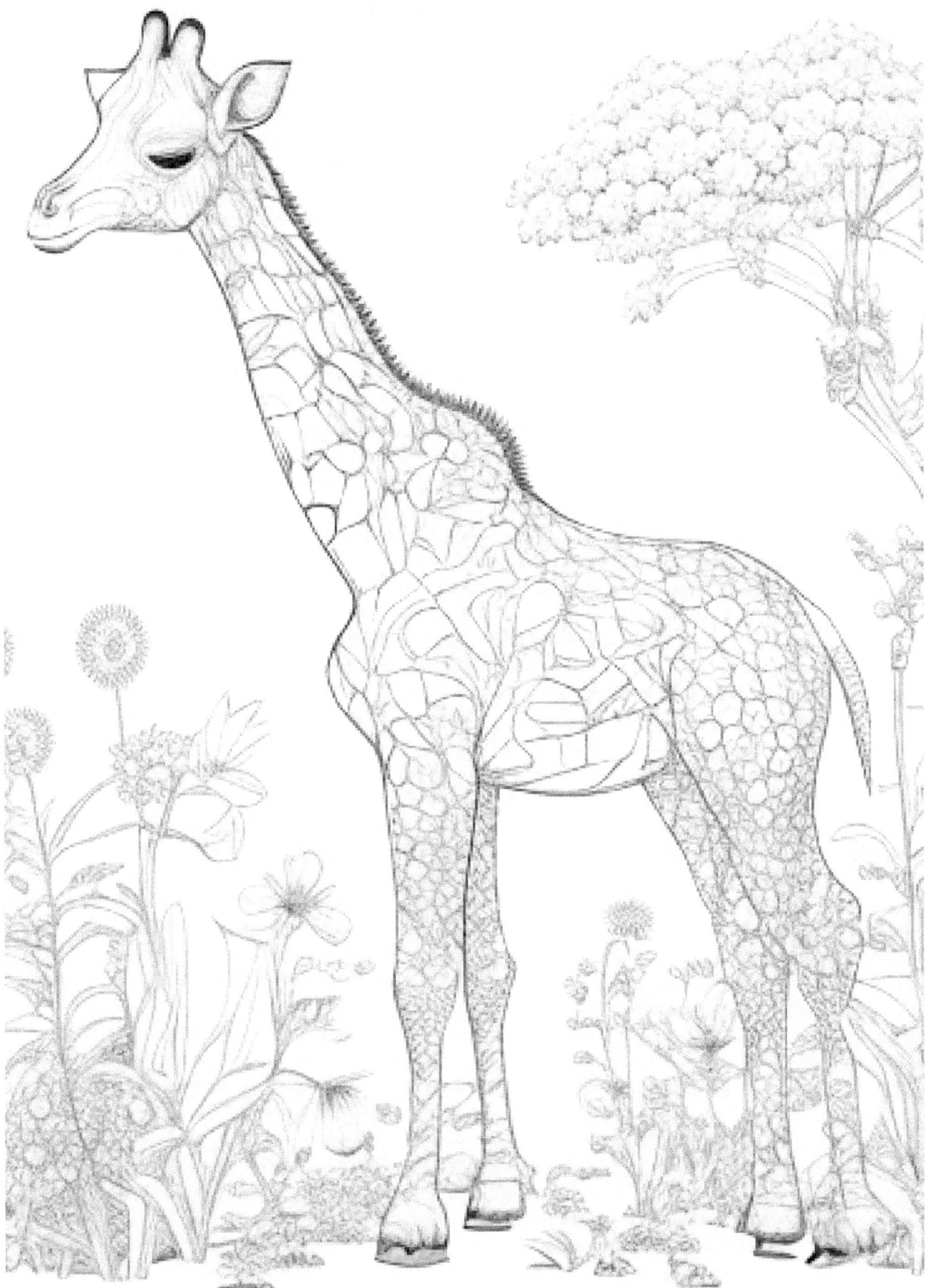

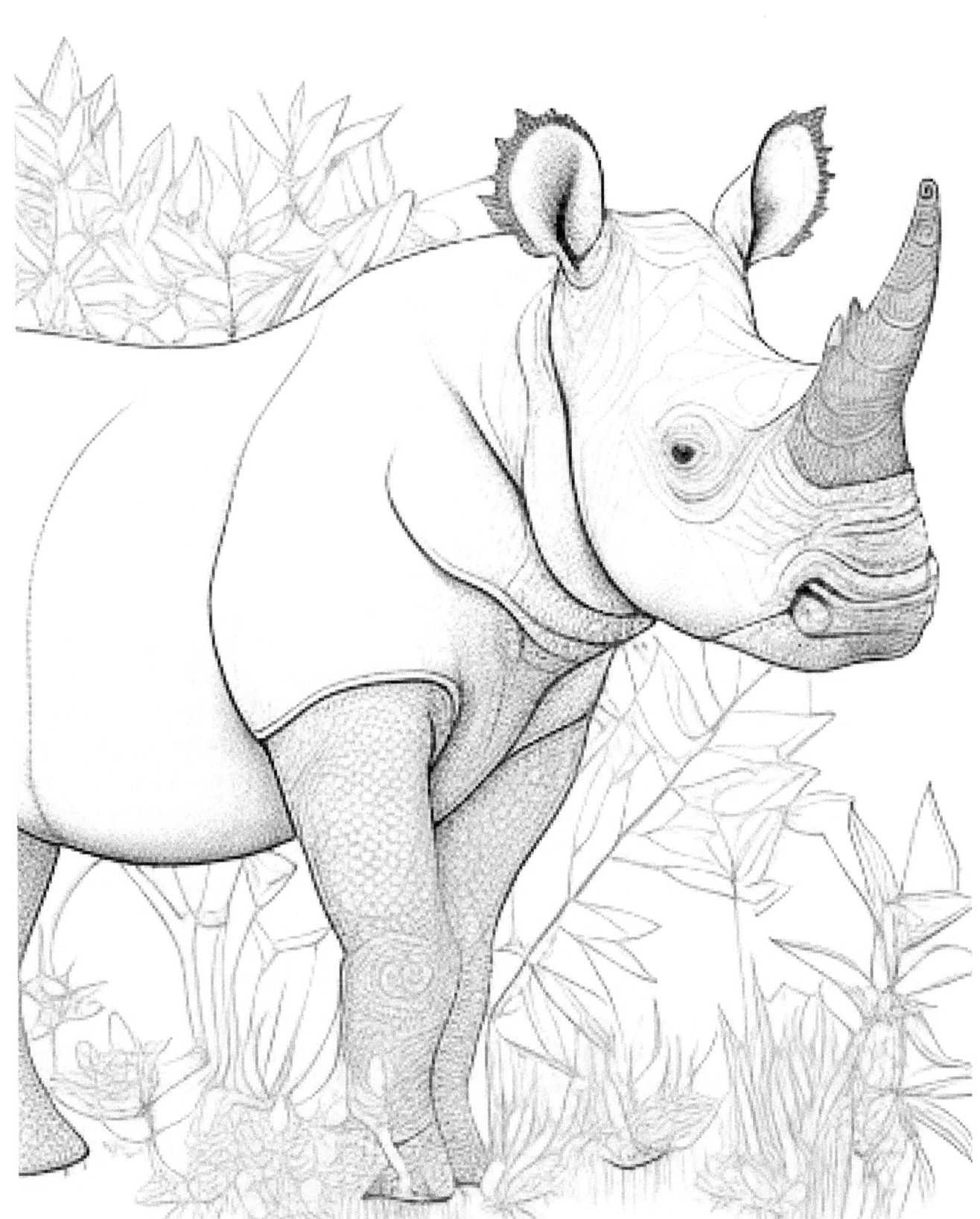

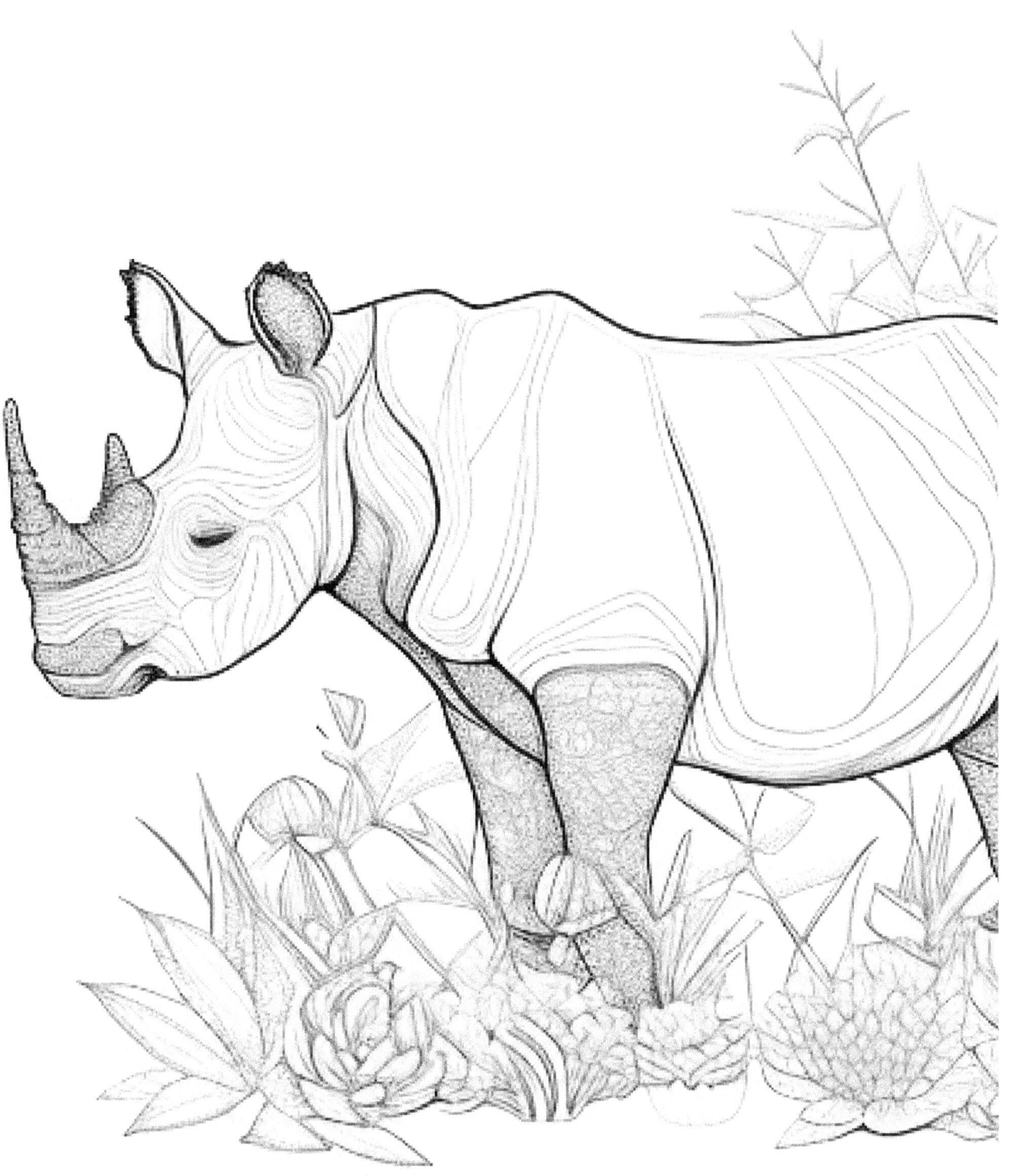

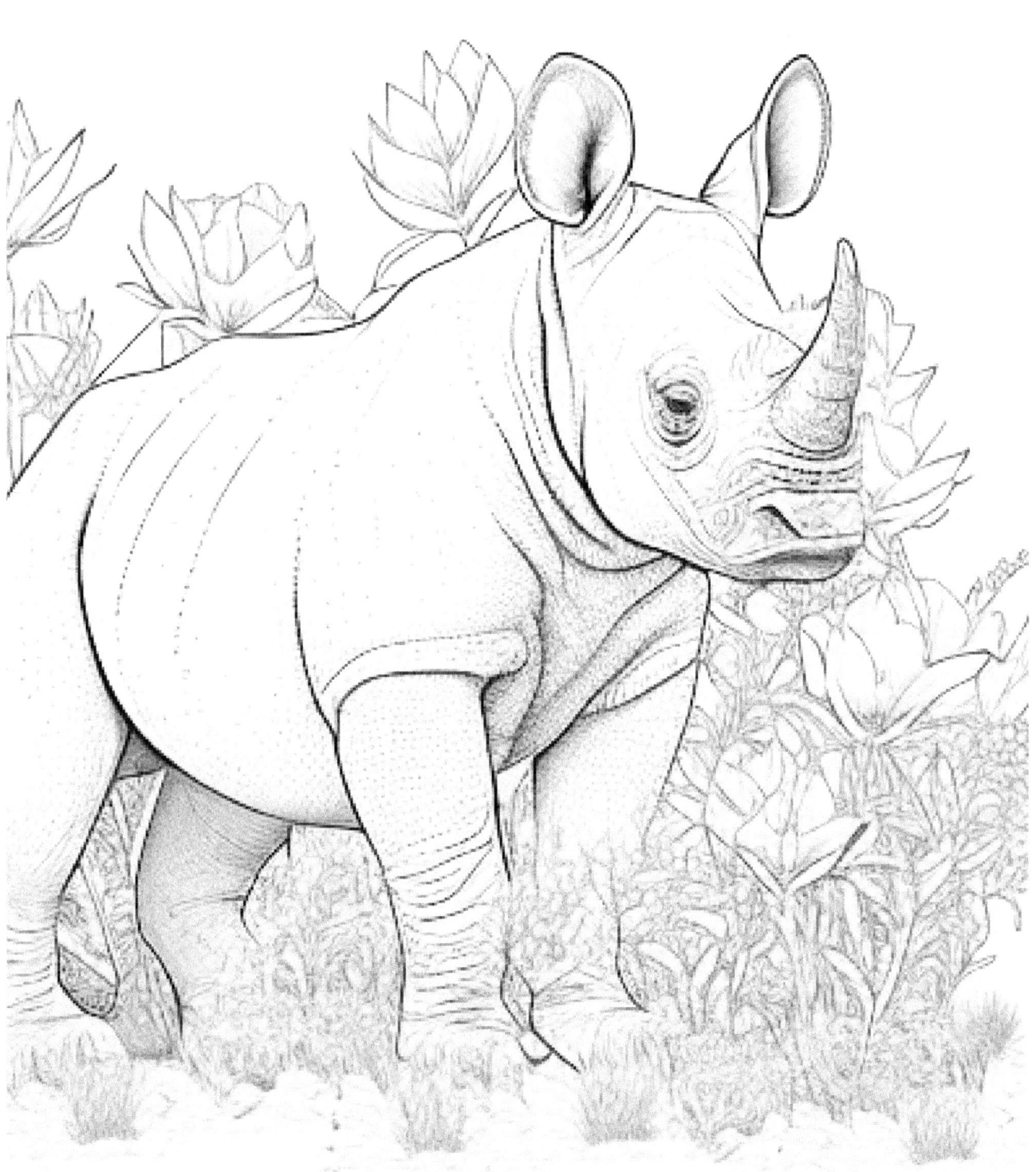

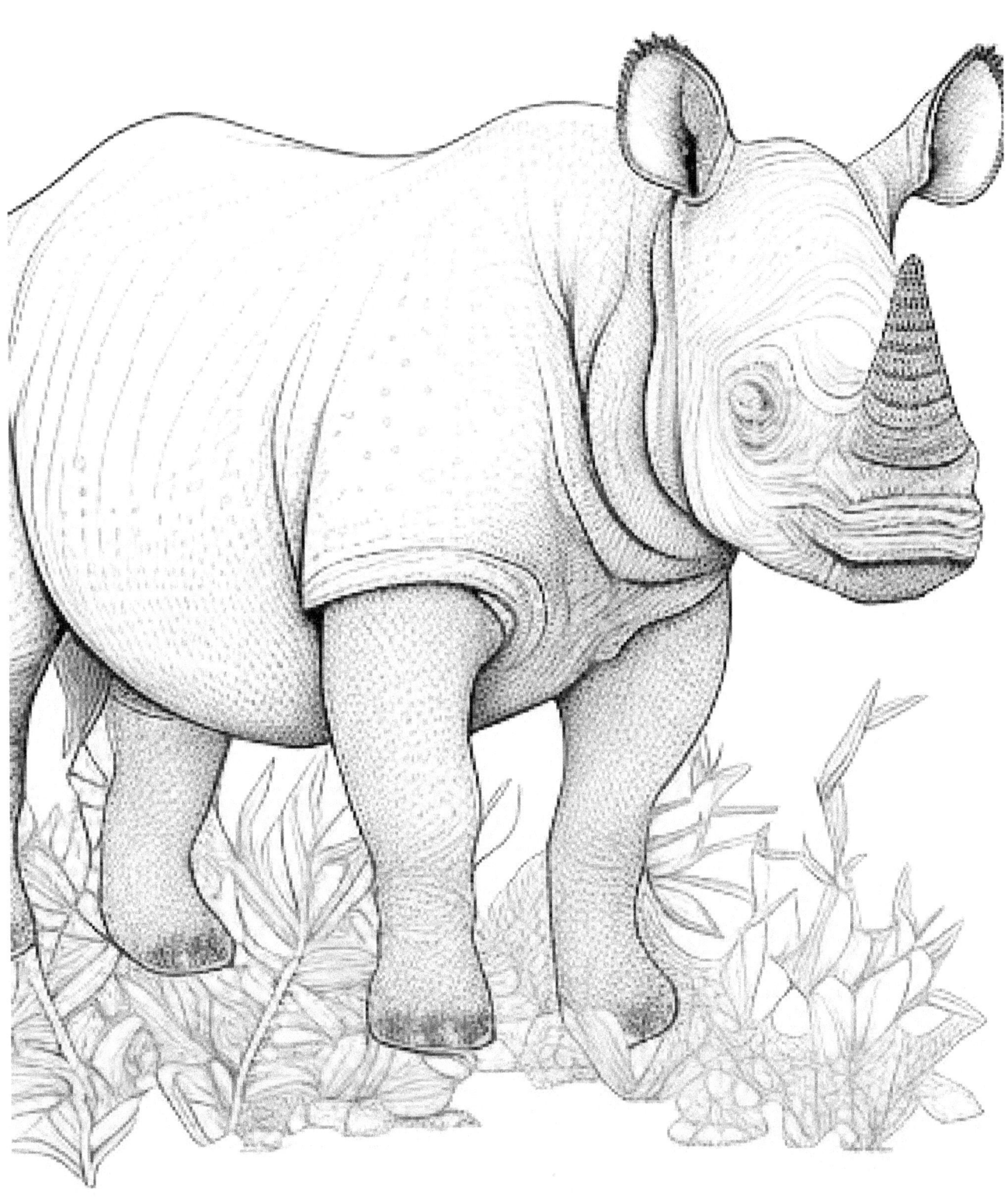

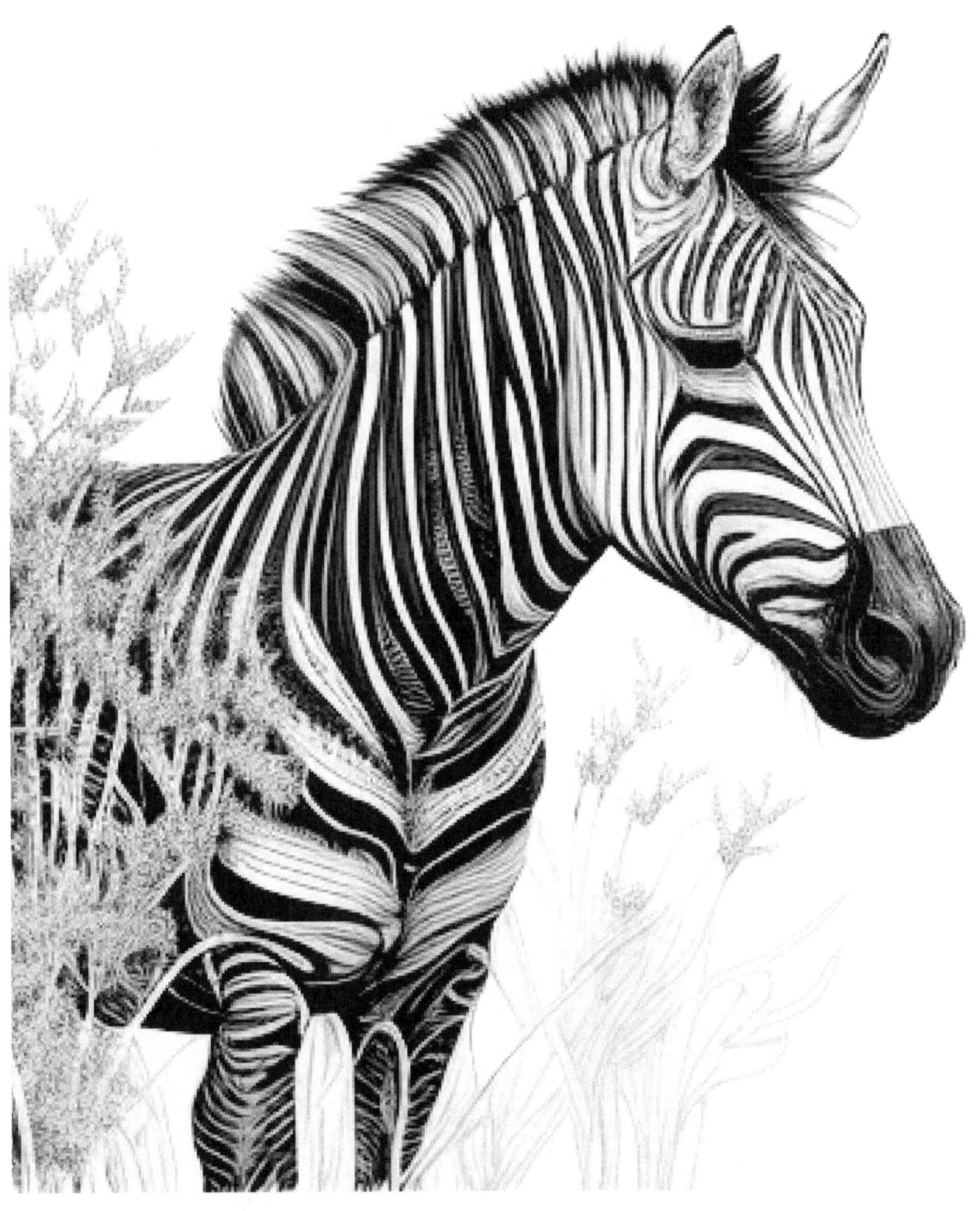

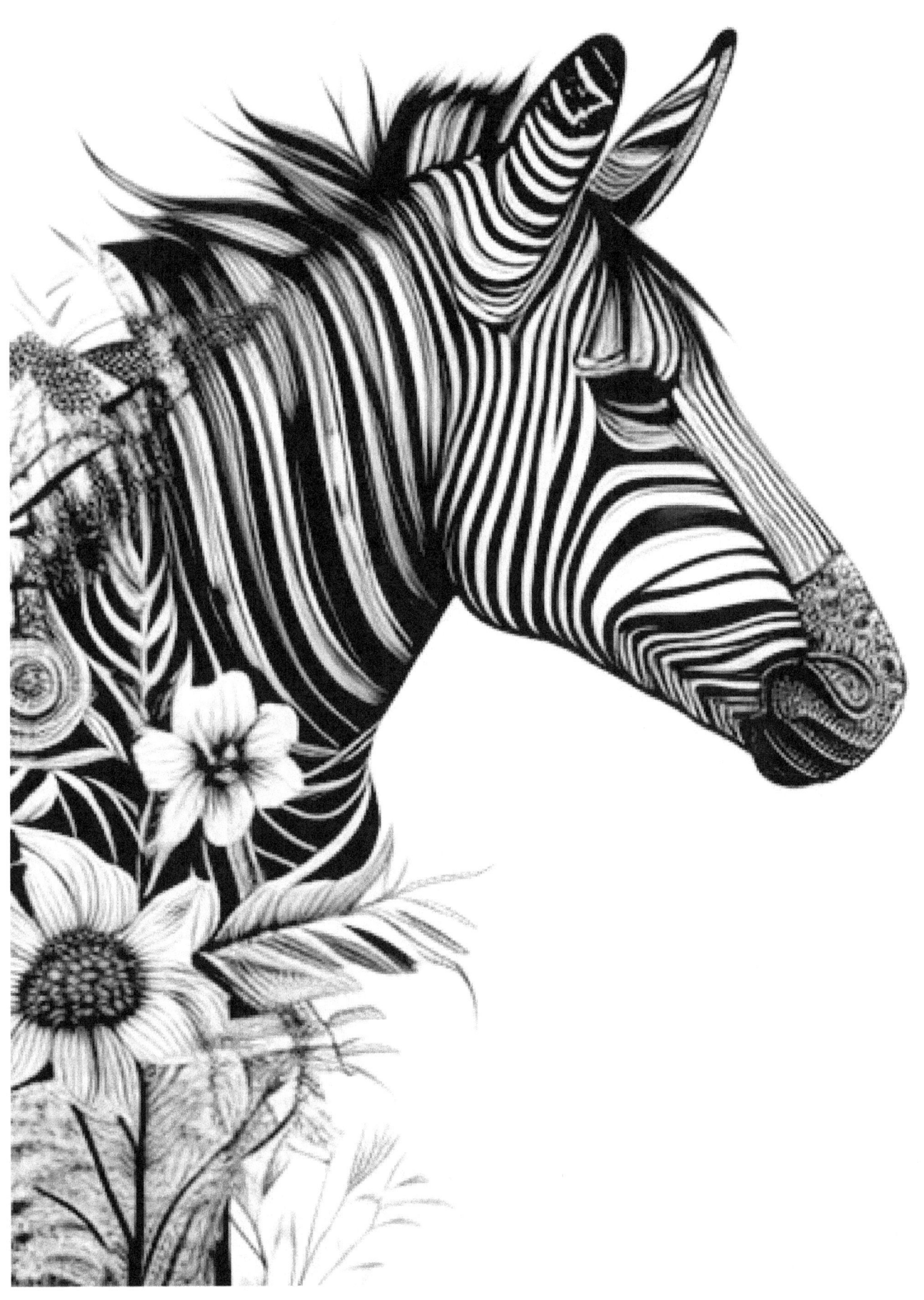

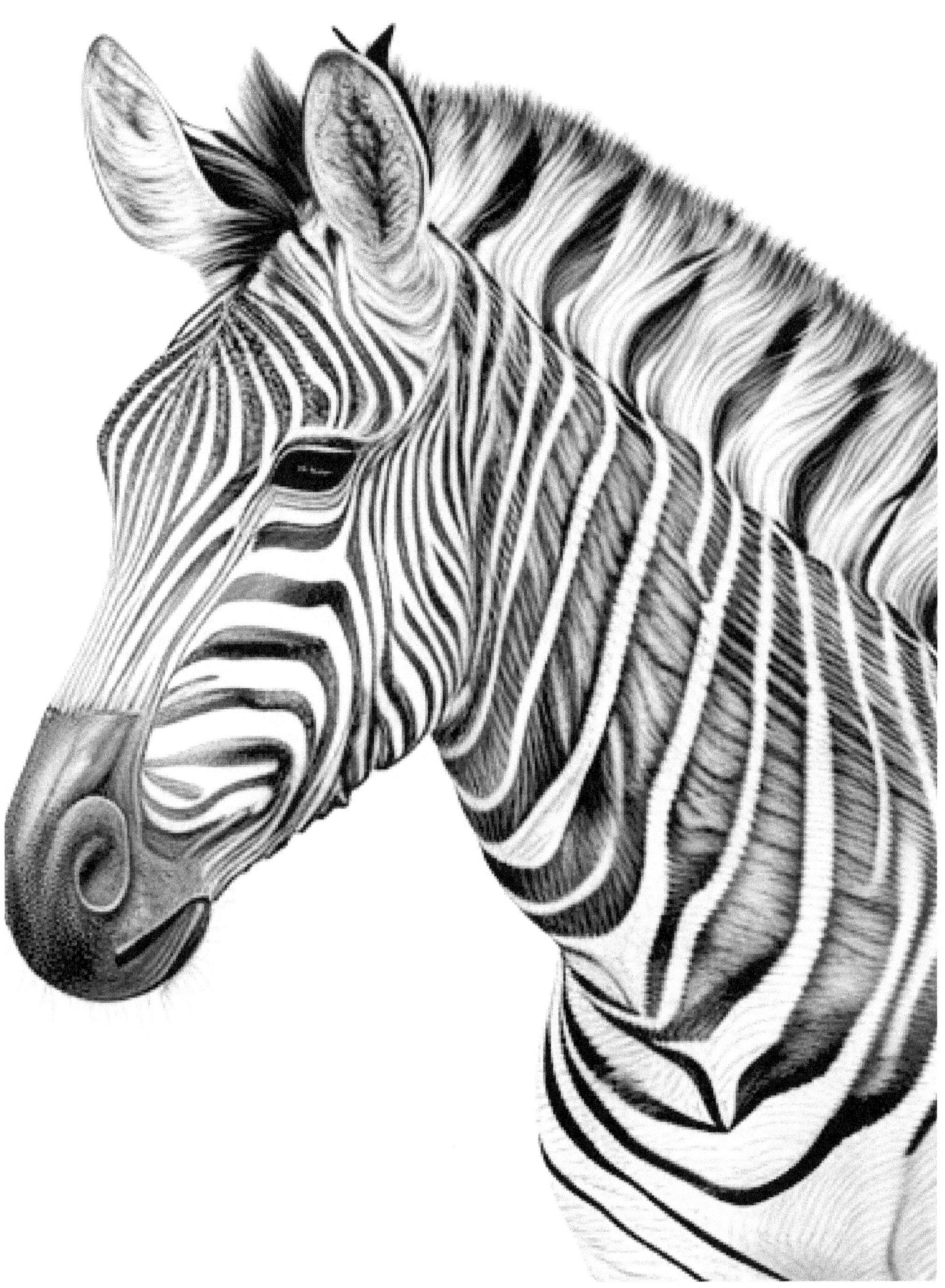

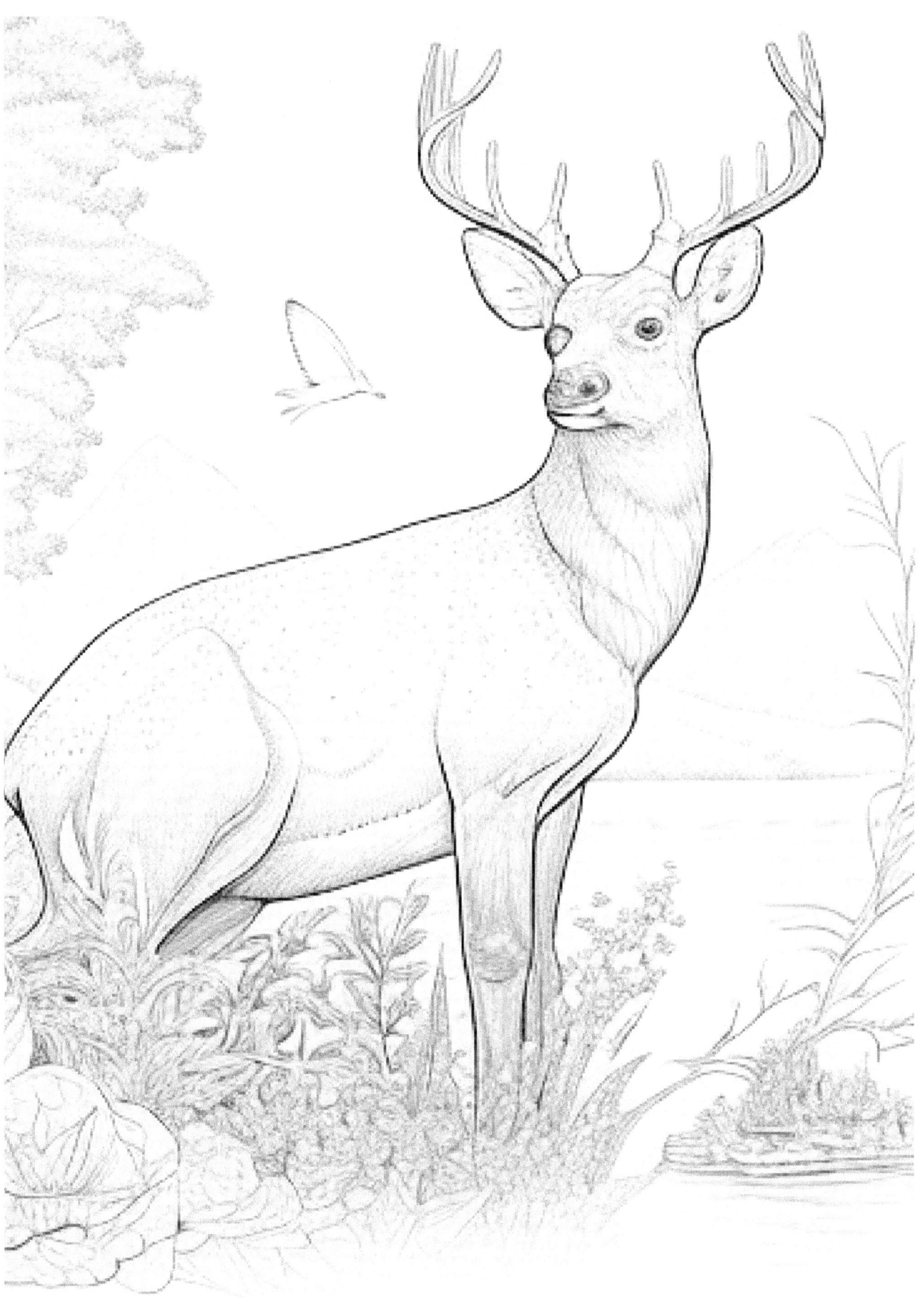

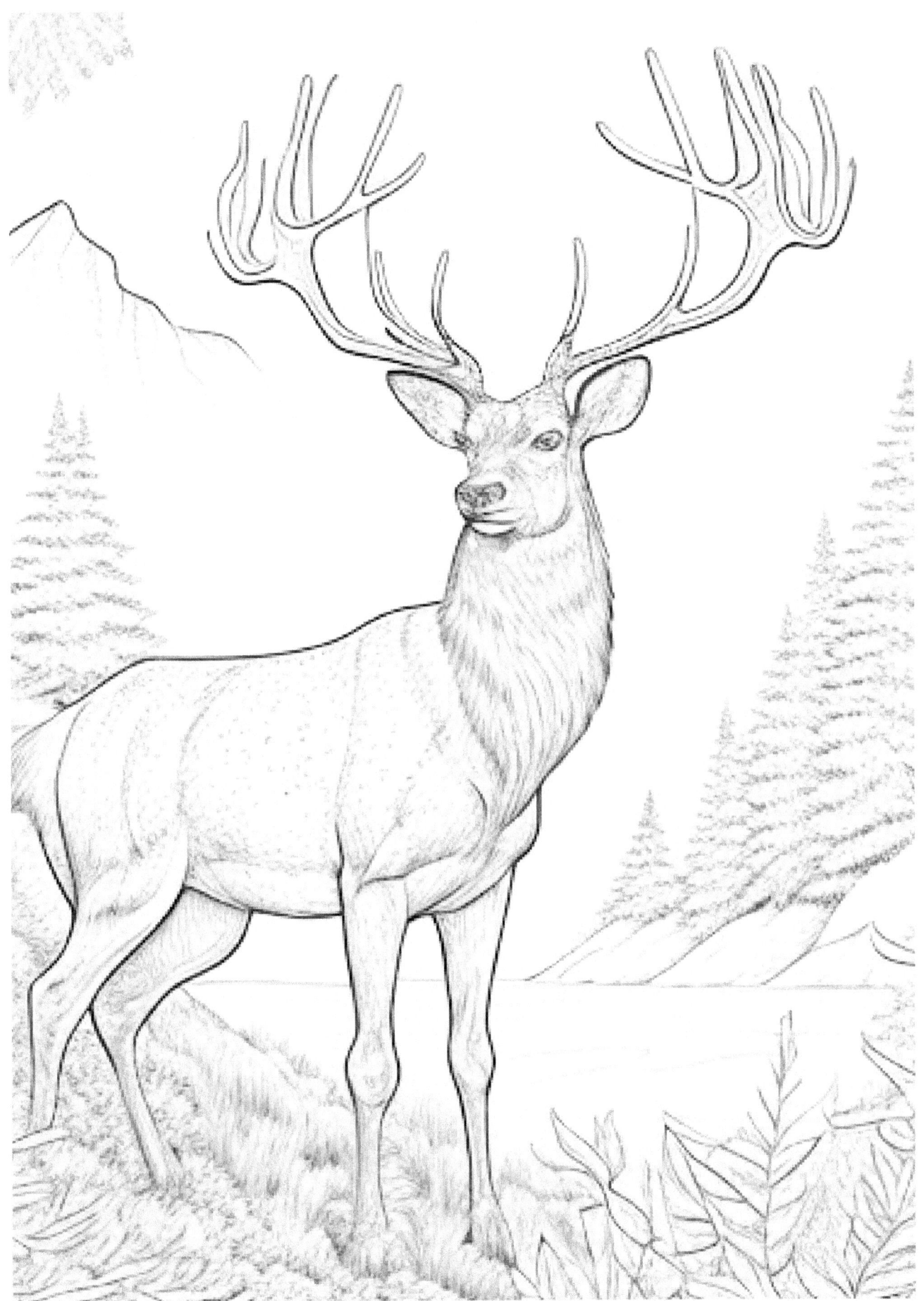

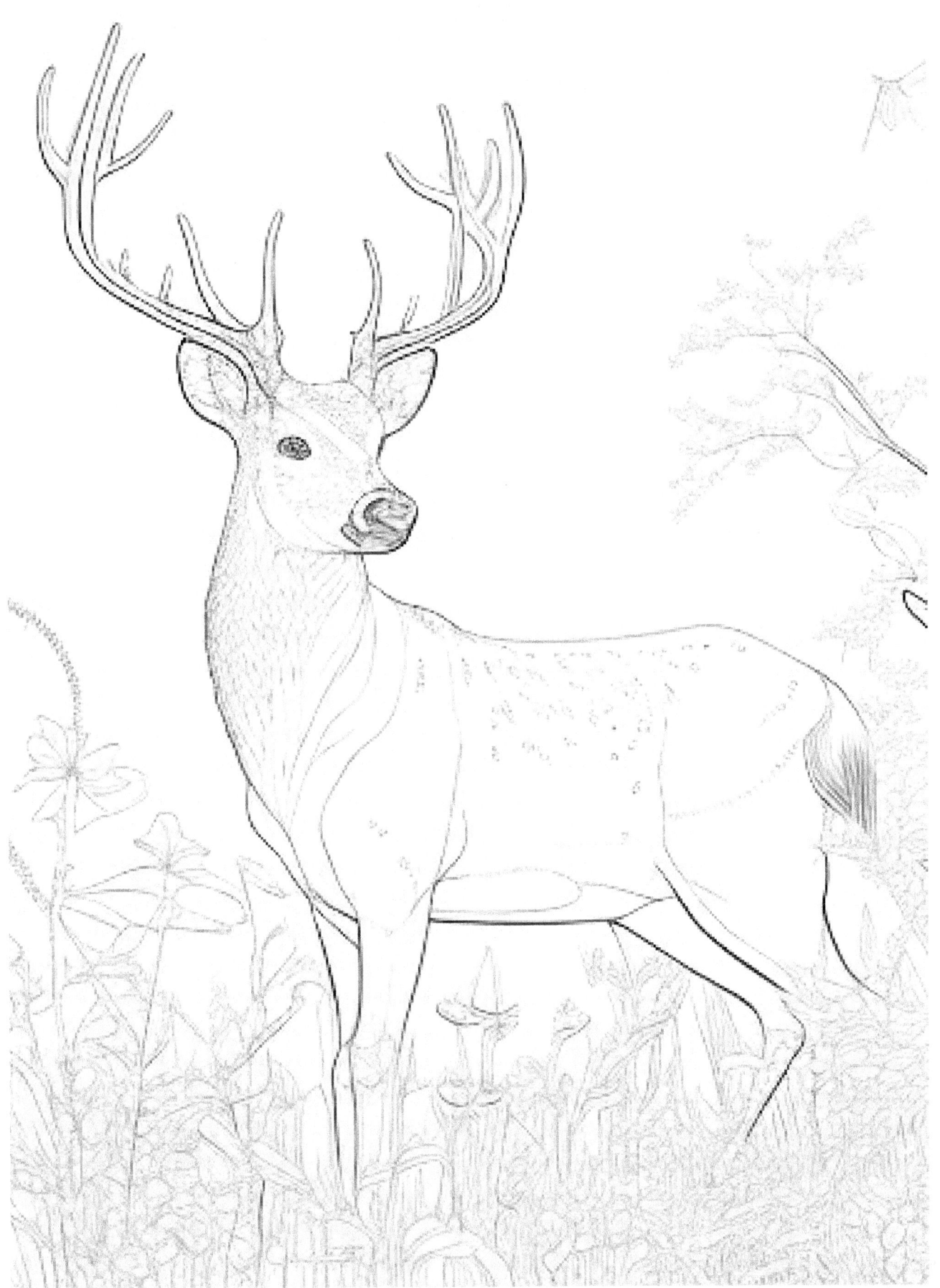